SOUNDS

WASSILY KANDINSKY

SOUNDS

TRANSLATED AND WITH AN INTRODUCTION BY

ELIZABETH R. NAPIER

New Haven and London, Yale University Press

TO DAVID

Published with assistance from
the foundation established in
memory of F. B. Adams, Jr.

Designed by James J. Johnson
and set in Helvetica type.
Printed in the United States of America by
The Vail-Ballou Press, Binghamton, N.Y.

Photographs of the woodcuts from *Klänge* courtesy
of The Solomon R. Guggenheim Museum,
New York (Robert E. Mates, photographer)

Library of Congress Cataloging in Publication Data

Kandinsky, Wassily, 1866–1944.
  Sounds.

  Translation of Klänge.
  English and German.
  Bibliography: p.
    1. Kandinsky, Wassily, 1866–1944. I. Napier,
Elizabeth R., 1950– II. Title.
NE1156.5.K36A4 1980   769.92'4   80–26628
ISBN 0–300-02510-6
ISBN 0–300-02664-1 (pbk.)

10   9   8   7

CONTENTS

CONTENTS

PREFACE

Wassily Kandinsky's *Klänge* is one of the earliest and most interesting texts in the history of twentieth-century art. Composed during the seminal years of Kandinsky's emergence into abstraction, it is central to an understanding of his *oeuvre* and to the larger concern with nonobjective art that characterized the early part of the century. The book was published in 1912 by Piper Verlag of Munich in a limited edition of 345 copies and was never reissued. Despite its importance, it has remained virtually unknown to modern readers and critics. It is here reprinted for the first time in its entirety.

Of the fifty-six woodcuts that figured in the Piper edition, twelve were printed in color. These woodcuts appear here in black and white. In all other respects, the present book has been designed to reproduce, in a reduced format, the most salient features of the original work. For the reader interested in the exact appearance of the German text, Hans Konrad Roethel's *Kandinsky: Das graphische Werk* (Cologne: M. DuMont Schauberg, 1970) contains facsimile reprints of a number of pages from *Klänge*.

This is the first complete translation into English.

I have been assisted in my work by a number of persons whom I particularly wish to thank, among them, Max Bill, Jelena Hahl, Nina Kandinsky, Breon Mitchell, Frank Ryder, and the staffs of the Bodleian, Houghton, and Middlebury College libraries. Editors at Piper Verlag and Denoël extended helpful suggestions. Grateful acknowledgment is made to A.D.A.G.P., Paris, which allowed the translation and reissuing of this work, and to the Solomon R. Guggenheim Museum, which kindly provided prints from its copy of *Klänge*.

Grants from the Faculty Research Fund of Middlebury College helped make aspects of this work possible.

All translations from French to English are by Barbara Ryder.

INTRODUCTION

In the past, the painter was looked at askance when he wrote—even if it were letters. He was practically expected to eat with a brush rather than with a fork.[1]

In 1938, recalling the publication of *Klänge*, Kandinsky spoke of it as "a small example of synthetic work":

This is, for me, a "change of instrument"—the palette to one side and the typewriter in its place. I use the word "instrument" because the force which motivates my work remains unchanged, an "inner drive." And it is this very drive which calls for a frequent change of instrument.[2]

For Kandinsky, 1908–14 were crucial years of transition and experimentation. By 1909, he had begun the composition of *Klänge*; by summer of that year, he was exhibiting in his painting the first decisive signs of a turning away from objective representation and a growing interest in abstraction. As the orientation of Kandinsky's work shifted, a change occurred in his compositional procedure: the logical demands of an extrinsic subject matter gradually began to give way to an organizational theory founded upon inherent properties of color and form. In principle, the transition was from an "absolute" mode of composition that derived from sources outside the work to one that arose from

---

1. "Autrefois on regardait le peintre 'de travers', quand il écrivait—même si c'était des lettres. On voulait presque qu'il mange non pas à la fourchette, mais avec un pinceau." Wassily Kandinsky, "Mes gravures sur bois," *XXe Siècle* 1, no. 3 (1938): 31.

2. "Ce qui est pour moi un 'changement d'instrument'—la palette de côté et à sa place la machine à écrire. Je dis 'instrument', parce que la force qui me pousse à mon travail reste toujours la même, c'est-à-dire une 'pression intérieure'. Et c'est elle qui me demande de changer souvent d'instrument." Kandinsky, "Mes gravures sur bois," p. 31.

the artistic materials themselves and the way these materials produced and modified their own terms of organization. Kandinsky expressed this theory succinctly in 1919:

> Every work chooses its own form and is subject to inner necessity alone. Every element of form has its absolute physical effect (= value); the construction chooses among these media in such a fashion as to turn absolute value to relative value, so that, for example, warm becomes cold and sharp dull.[3]

The poems of *Klänge*, written during the seminal years of Kandinsky's residence in Munich, attest to the growth of this transformational urge. On the levels of both form and theme, they afford insight into the artist's attitude toward abstraction and his commitment to the complex energies of redefinition and change.[4]

Jean Arp, who with Hugo Ball and the Zurich Dadaists recognized in Kandinsky one of the forebears of the new artistic movement,[5] proclaimed his indebtedness to *Klänge* in an essay of 1951. He called the work "one of the extraordinary, great books." He saw in the poetry compositions in perpetual motion, forms en route from an earthly to a spiritual realm:

3. "Jedes Werk wählt sich seine Form und unterliegt nur der inneren Notwendigkeit. Jedes Formelement hat seine absolute physische Wirkung (= Wert); die Konstruktion wählt unter diesen Mitteln so, daß sie den absoluten Wert zu einem relativen macht, so daß zum Beispiel Warmes kalt wird und Spitziges stumpf." Wassily Kandinsky, "Selbstcharakteristik," *Das Kunstblatt* 3, no. 6 (1919): 174. Unless otherwise noted, translations from German to English are my own.

4. That *Klänge* was regarded by Kandinsky himself as an expression of the artist's transitional years is suggested in a passage from "Mes gravures sur bois," p. 31.

> Dans ces bois comme dans le reste—bois et poèmes—on retrouve les traces de mon développement du "figuratif" à l' "abstrait" ("concret" d'après ma terminologie—plus exacte et plus expressive que l'habituelle—à mon avis du moins).

> [In these woodcuts, as in the rest—woodcuts and poems—can be found traces of my development from the "figurative" to the "abstract" (the "concrete" according to my terminology—which is, in my opinion at least, more precise and more expressive than the usual).]

Kandinsky executed his first abstract work around 1909; by 1914 the figurative element had virtually disappeared from his painting.

5. Ball, in particular, was inspired by Kandinsky's example. "When we said Kandinsky and Picasso," he recalls, "we meant not painters but priests; not craftsmen, but creators of new worlds and new paradises." *Flight out of Time: A Dada Diary, 1910–21, 1924–* , ed. John Elderfield, trans. Ann Raimes (New York: Viking, 1974), p. 7 (originally published as *Die Flucht aus der Zeit* [Munich: Duncker & Humblot, 1927]). "There was no art form that he had tried," Ball wrote of Kandinsky, "without taking completely new paths, undeterred by derision and scorn. In him, word, color, and sound worked in rare harmony . . . " (p. 8); "in poetry too he is the first to

These works breathe the secrets of eternal and unexplored depths. Forms arise, as powerful as talking mountains. Sulphur and poppy stars blossom at the lips of the sky.[6]

The poems of *Klänge*, Arp noted, exhibit a recurrent concern with transformation; their design suggests a continual interchange of appearing and dissolution, a world in explicit transfiguration:

> Through the poetry of Kandinsky the reader is witness to the eternal cycle, the becoming and the disappearing, the transformation of this world.[7]

The poems also reveal Kandinsky's formal means for the expression of this change: his experimentation with the construction of words and his attention to modes of repetition and variation in dialogues and chants. These lexical and compositional procedures are augmented by patterns of narrative in the poetry which move from situations of stasis to those of ongoing process. The result is a series of poems that suggest a world of multiple interpretative possibilities, and in which perception figures as the central, crucial form of engagement with the real.

Kandinsky's interest in types of patterning and variation is pervasive in *Klänge*. The simplest form of patterning, basic repetition, recurs as a fundamental syntactical and metrical device in his poems. In *Erde*, syntactical repetition and assonance (of the key terms, "schwer" and "Erde") are utilized to slow the rhythm of the language and emphasize the gross, elemental quality of man's labor with the earth. The uncomplicated incantatory rhythms of a poem such as *Tisch* ("Es war ein langer Tisch. Oh, ein langer, langer Tisch") stress, in similar fashion, Kandinsky's awareness of the primitive (and here notably childlike) attraction of pure reiteration.

---

present purely spiritual processes. . . . Nowhere else, even among the futurists, has anyone attempted such a daring purification of language" (p. 234). Kandinsky, though he did not become directly involved with the Dadaists, was a driving force behind the new group in Zurich: his paintings were included in Dadaist exhibitions and his poems recited at Dada soirées through 1919. Ball's diaries and his 1917 lecture on Kandinsky (trans. Christopher Middleton, in *Flight out of Time*, pp. 222–34) attest repeatedly to the strength of his influence.

6. "Il passe dans ces morceaux un souffle venu de fonds éternels et inexplorés. Des formes se lèvent, puissantes comme des montagnes parlantes. Des étoiles de soufre et de coquelicot fleurissent aux lèvres du ciel." Jean Arp, "Kandinsky, le poète," in *Wassily Kandinsky*, ed. Max Bill (Paris: Maeght, 1951), pp. 89–93. According to Kandinsky, Arp valued his copy of *Klänge* so highly that he would lend it to no one and forebade even his wife to read it. See Hans Konrad Roethel, *Kandinsky: Das graphische Werk* (Cologne: M. DuMont Schauberg, 1970), p. 448.

7. "Par la poésie de Kandinsky, nous assistons au cycle éternel, au devenir et à la disparition, à la transformation de ce monde." Arp, p. 90.

Although in both *Erde* and *Tisch* repetition serves to stabilize and to simplify an already circumscribed universe, the reduplication of phrases and single words occasionally evokes resonances of a more complex nature. In *Offen*, the mysterious quality of the poem's landscape derives from heavily rhythmical cycles of sounds which, in imitation of the recurring seasons, approach and recede from the deep, central *o* of "Rohre." Syntactical repetition in *Hymnus*, accentuated by strangely monotonous patterns of rhyme and meter, suggests an elemental process of a similarly enigmatic type. Here, as in the poem *Klänge*, the appearance of opaque symbols creates the effect of an impenetrable surface of mystery. Often the device of repeating affords access into the realm of the alogical and the absurd. The struggle for precision reflected in the "etwas, etwas, etwas" ["a little, little, little"] refrain of *Anders* points to the limitations of a traditionally quantitative appraisal of reality. The frenzied incantations of the characters in *Bunte Wiese*, the verbal concatenation of *Blick und Blitz*, and the "deng, deng, deng, deng, deng" of the bell which concludes the poem *Glocke* encourage a similar escape from the convention of logical resolution.[8]

Within such highly iterative structures, the appearance of variation is attended with particular formal and thematic significance. As repetitive patterns typically increase the connotative capacity of language, so in the poems of *Klänge* complex iterative patterns with variation are often used to move language away from the denotative into the domain of the abstract and suggestive:

> Language no longer functions as a keyboard, the word frees itself from the stocktaking of reality, and a combination of words . . . materializes into a thing that approaches painting and thus returns to that material form with which the painter is familiar. In short: the object here is not the elementary red, but the result of the artistic act.[9]

A tendency to unstring and manipulate the elements of language shows itself frequently in Kandinsky's *Klänge*. His poetry evinces a repeated interest in syntactical

---

8. Kandinsky also explores this point in *Über das Geistige in der Kunst:* "repetition . . . will not only tend to intensify the inner harmony [of a word] but also bring to light unsuspected spiritual properties of the word itself. Further than that, frequent repetition of a word . . . deprives the word of its original external meaning." *Concerning the Spiritual in Art*, trans. M. T. H. Sadler (New York: Dover, 1977), p. 15 (originally published as *Über das Geistige in der Kunst* [Munich: Piper Verlag, 1912]).

9. "Die Sprache hört auf, Tastatur zu sein, das Wort löst sich von der Bestandsaufnahme der Wirklichkeit, und eine Wortverbindung . . . materialisiert sich zu einem Ding, das dem Gemälde nahekommt und damit zu jener Stofflichkeit zurückkehrt, die dem Maler vertraut ist. Kurz: das Objekt ist hier nicht das elementare Rot,

jokes, in the unravelling and reassembling of words and phrases. Such activity reaffirms Kandinsky's central concern with the relationship between a pattern and its variation. Thus, in the poem *Vorhang*, the dissection of the verb *hängen* produces the absurd litany, "Der Vorhang hing"; the cumulative rhythm of the "Ein Stein" chant in *Bunte Wiese* operates with similar ridiculous effect. It is significant throughout that occurrence of variation does not in a conventional sense "unlock" the meaning of the pattern that it modifies: the "tin-ten" of the clock in *Unverändert* throws no logical light on the "Tinten" with which the Turk waters his little tree. The isolation of the symbolic sword and rope in the poem *Klänge* fails similarly to resolve the meaning of the actions in which these emblems participate. In drawing repeated formal notice to pattern, Kandinsky has, in effect, transferred interpretative weight from a language system affording possible denotative solutions to an abstract complex in which design attains dominant thematic significance.

Much as the language of *Klänge* asserts the syntactical importance of pattern and variation, so, on the level of narrative structure, interplay between pattern and modifier functions as a central organizing device in the poetry. Within the longer narrative poems, action of "plot" typically moves from a point of stasis, where a pattern is established, to a point at which that pattern has become modified through interpolation of an often irrational or absurd event. In poems such as *Hügel, Hoboe, Abenteuer,* and *Blätter*, quiet landscapes are "invaded" by men (or beasts) behaving in highly enigmatic ways. In *Hügel*, the blackness of the drummer introduces a new dimension into a previously simple landscape: "Wie gründlich erschöpft liegt er da, der schwarze Mann, lang gestreckt auf dem weißen Pfad, zwischen den Hügeln in allen Farben" ["As if utterly exhausted he lies there, the black man, all stretched out over the white path, among the hills of all colors"]. The blue man who rides his mysterious goat into the landscape of *Blätter* initiates a more radical revision of poetic scenery: the leaves fall from the tree and the flowers turn into red berries. Action, as in the poems *Fagott, Wasser,* and *Der Turm*, attains here the qualities of pure design—it consists of an alien pattern manifesting itself in an established landscape.

In many of the poems, formal changes in setting may be traced to a specific object or event. In *Fagott*, a line of crows flying across the sky induces a stilling of all activity: the orange-cloud disappears, the sky and town change color. The poem *Wasser* portrays the alterations of land and seascape effected by the physical and mental progress of the little thin red man. In *Der Turm*, the appearance of the woman provokes a similar

---

sondern Resultat der künstlerischen Handlung." Hans Platschek, *Dichtung moderner Maler* (Wiesbaden: Limes, 1956), p. 8.

rearrangement of setting: "Sie setzte sich neben ihm und alle Pilze verschwanden" ["She sat down beside him and all the mushrooms disappeared"].

The verses of *Klänge*, as the poem *Das Weiche* attests, describe a world in constant formal tension. In nearly all the poems an act of transformation occurs or hovers in the background. Revolutionary or social transition is not the primary area of concern, although Kandinsky may move tentatively in that direction in poems such as *Fagott, Glocke,* and *Doch Noch?*; his interest resides, rather, in the more abstract context of formal relationships, in the manner in which a created artistic reality may be modified and transformed.

In a world in which change has become a factor of relevance, man's capacity to adjust to and understand his environment depends critically upon his ability to perceive. For Kandinsky, moments of impotence and confusion are typically moments of not seeing. The barrier in the poem *Blick* thus impedes not only vision but a potential moment of human contact. A similar dilemma is described in *Käfig*. Here, the narrator's inability to apprehend his surroundings has been reified as an invisible cage which arrests his forward movement. The singing man of the poem *Lied*, deprived of both hearing and seeing, is surrounded in like fashion by a constricting "ring." Other impediments to communication recur intermittently throughout *Klänge*. In *Frühling* and *Doch Noch?* silence becomes a pervasive metaphor for the alienation and despair of the speakers. In *Frühling* the air has explicitly ceased to carry sound; it no longer serves as a medium for communication. The result is a peculiar stasis of meaning, in which the poem's central symbols—the rotting cross and the lightning—remain uninterpreted and obscure.

Reality, as a line from the poem *Anders* admits, is not easy to see. Indeed, it is the central function of visual evidence in *Klänge* to bring into question what we regard as real. Throughout Kandinsky's poetry, unusual events or settings are treated as nothing out of the ordinary: the extinguished flash of lightning and the disappearing bench in *Unverändert* constitute the continually shifting categories of one speaker's existence, and "everybody" knows the giant cloud in *Das* that resembles a cauliflower. Objects of landscape may also take on troubling and indefinable symbolic resonances, as in *Frühling* and *Ausgang*, where the vision of the cross and the dry scrape of the stick deliberately begin to veer off into the realm of the surreal. The detachment of landscape elements in the poem *Klänge* operates in similar fashion to isolate and intensify symbolic possibilities at the expense of empirical probability.

Often the boundaries between what is perceived and what is not perceived tend to dissolve: "Der Fisch ging immer tiefer. Ich sah ihn aber noch. Ich sah ihn nicht mehr.

Ich sah ihn noch, wenn ich ihn nicht sehen konnte" ["The fish went deeper and deeper. But I could still see it. I couldn't see it anymore. I could still see it, when I couldn't see it"] (*Einiges*); "Und die grünen Ohren! / Waren sie grün? Oder doch nicht? Oder doch?" ["And the green ears! / Were they green? Or weren't they? Or were they?"] (*Kreide und Russ*). In *Klänge*, Kandinsky toys with the notion of a reality which is purely speculative, in which, as in *Kreide und Russ*, one may choose whether one prefers to have seen a black face with white lips or a white face with black lips. The frequency of the conditional "perhaps" in his poetry suggests the complex potential of the sensory in Kandinsky's world. Is reality determined by the wishes of the observer (as is the shape of the hills in *Hügel* or the presence of fish in *Einiges*) or is it, in fact, as the poem *Anders* implies, merely an arbitrary way of ordering experience: "Es war vielleicht auch anders" ["But then again maybe it was different"]? The ability to respond to enigmatic or paradoxical settings (as the "little round flat hill" in *Hoboe* or the tree, in *Fagott*, that does not move with the wind) presupposes an expressly untraditional method of seeing. In constructing landscapes of "alternatives," Kandinsky hints at a reality which is unfixed, in which perception becomes of paramount importance. The poem *Sehen* pronounces the necessity of a shift in point of view, a radical commitment to "the art of seeing."[10] The issue here is not one of bringing a logical order to an illogical universe; indeed, the "white leaps" of *Sehen* and the unexpected symbol of the tree and apples that resolves the poem *Käfig* point directly away from conventional or static notions of interpretation. In *Klänge*, as well as in Kandinsky's paintings of the same period, form and content enforce a view of reality that places implicit faith in the activity of transformation, that entertains and participates in the crucial possibilities of change.[11]

It would be unwise and unfortunate to disregard certain facts (one might call them "events") which surround us and which push us toward the freedom that is synthesis. Too bad for those who wish to block the way.[12]

10. The expression is El Lissitzky's: "Das Sehen ist nämlich auch eine K[unst]." "K[unst] und Pangeometrie," in *Europa-Almanach*, vol. 1, ed. Carl Einstein and Paul Westheim (1925; reprint ed., Nendeln, Liechtenstein: Kraus, 1973), p. 103.

11. It is interesting to note, for example, in many of Kandinsky's *Improvisations* of 1911–12, and in *Komposition V* (1911) and *Mit dem schwarzen Bogen* (1912) in particular, a frequent tendency to superscribe large formalized areas of landscape with winding or diagonal black lines. See Will Grohmann, *Wassily Kandinsky: Life and Work,* trans. Norbert Guterman (London: Thames & Hudson, 1959), pp. 103–59.

12. "C'est imprudent et malheureux de fermer les yeux sur quelques faits (on pourrait dire 'événements') qui nous entourent et qui nous poussent vers la liberté de la synthèse. Tant pis pour ceux qui veulent barrer la route." Kandinsky, "Mes gravures sur bois," p. 31.

A Note on *Klänge*

A note by Kandinsky in the publisher's prospectus for *Klänge* indicates that Kandinsky began the composition of the prose-poems around 1909–10.[13] The woodcuts date from 1907. It is difficult to trace the beginnings of *Klänge* with more precision. In the Salon d'Automne in Paris in 1910, Kandinsky placed on exhibition four woodcuts "pour un album avec texte"; later that year, six woodcuts "zu einem Album mit Text" appeared in an exhibition of the Neue Künstlervereinigung in Munich; another reference to an album accompanied by text occurs in the catalogue of an exhibition in Berlin in March 1912. Letters to Gabriele Münter in the summer of 1911 indicate that Kandinsky was working assiduously on the woodcuts for *Klänge*, and by August he wrote that the work ("mein Album") was nearly complete.

The book was originally designed for publication in Moscow: a maquette for a Russian edition (which Kandinsky may have planned during his stay in Odessa in December of 1910) is in the Gabriele Münter Foundation in the Städtische Galerie, Munich.[14] This original version of *Klänge*, which contained seventeen poems in Russian, was to have been published in 1911 by Vladimir Izdebsky, a sculptor acquaintance of Kandinsky and organizer of two major international exhibitions of Western avant-garde art in Odessa in 1909–11. The book never materialized.

On September 12, 1912, Kandinsky signed the contract to publish with Piper Verlag of Munich. The book appeared in November in a single edition of three hundred signed and forty-five unsigned copies; the sale price was fixed at thirty marks. The agreement included mention of a possible second printing of *Klänge*, to be considered one or two years after the publication of the first edition. This version, with a price of approximately three marks, was to have been presented in a reduced format with a selection of the smaller woodcuts. It did not appear.

13. "Alle 'Prosagedichte,' " wrote Kandinsky, "habe ich im Laufe der letzten drei Jahre geschrieben. Die Holzschnitte gehen bis in das Jahr 1907 hinauf." ["I wrote all of the prose-poems in the course of the last three years. The woodcuts go back to the year 1907."] See Roethel, p. 445. I am indebted throughout this section to Roethel's researches into the publishing background of *Klänge*.

Kandinsky's poetic activity dated from his childhood. "Like many children and young people," he recalled, "I attempted to write poetry which sooner or later I tore up." *Reminiscences,* trans. Mrs. Robert L. Herbert, in *Modern Artists on Art: Ten Unabridged Essays,* ed. Robert L. Herbert (Englewood Cliffs, N.J.: Prentice-Hall, 1964), pp. 19–44 (originally published as "Rückblicke," in *Kandinsky, 1901–1913* [Berlin: Der Sturm, 1913]). Drawing, Kandinsky maintained, eventually "released" him from this condition of personal doubt (p.27). By the time of *Klänge*, he was to synthesize the two creative processes which he then regarded as separate and conflicting.

14. A full comparison of the German and Russian editions of *Klänge* is currently being undertaken by Dr. Jelena Hahl, who kindly provided me with detailed information on her research. Her study will be published in the Roethel/Hahl edition of Kandinsky's writings (in progress).

The original *Klänge* contains thirty-eight poems and fifty-six woodcuts, twelve of which are full-page color prints. The poems are set in bold type on handmade Dutch paper. The book measures 11¼ inches square. It is bound in a dark red pasteboard cover and has a spine of purple linen. On the front and back covers a small vignette by Kandinsky is impressed in gold.

Though there was some disagreement about its popular reception,[15] *Klänge* is now regarded as one of the most significant artist's books of the twentieth century. *Klänge* has its roots in a period of radical change: conceived during the period of Kandinsky's movement toward abstraction, it is a work which both verbally and visually insists on the energy of nonobjective form. The poems and woodcuts of *Klänge* exhibit a repeated experimentation with the limits of the conventional objective world: the poems are alternately narrative and expressive in quality; the woodcuts—which, as a medium, were of special importance in Kandinsky's emergence into abstraction[16]—range from early Jugendstil-inspired (and still highly representational) designs to vignettes that are purely abstract in form.

Because Kandinsky's *Klänge* is a rare example of a work in which text and illustrations have been executed by the same artist, it poses special questions to the literary critic concerned with the relationship of illustration to text. The case of *Klänge* is particularly interesting because, in the transposition of poems from the proposed Russian edition into the German edition, the original order of the woodcuts was not adhered to. How, then, should these works of visual art be viewed? Are they illustrations of the text in the conventional sense or do they in some way modify our definition of the word *illustration*? The relationship of prints to poems in *Klänge* is, perhaps, more fundamental than is usual in an illustrated book: it lies in the conceptual unity between visual art and text, in the peculiar tension between representation and abstraction that characterizes both artistic forms.

15. The book, later lauded by Arp and the Zurich Dadaists, was unfavorably reviewed by Hans Tietze in *Die Graphischen Künste* 37 (1913): 15–16. In his article, Tietze commended the theoretical premises of *Klänge* but expressed serious reservations about the poetry and art, which he saw as unsuccessful embodiments of those theories. Piper and Kandinsky, too, held different views of the book's success. Piper wrote to Kandinsky in 1914 that fewer than one hundred copies of *Klänge* had been sold and for that reason, presumably, did not bring out a second edition. However, Kandinsky maintained in "Mes gravures sur bois" and elsewhere that the volume had been bought up quickly.

16. See Kenneth Lindsay, "Graphic Art in Kandinsky's Oeuvre," in *Prints: Thirteen Illustrated Essays on the Art of the Print*, ed. Carl Zigrosser (London: Peter Owen, 1963), pp. 235–47; Peg Weiss, *Kandinsky in Munich: The Formative Jugendstil Years* (Princeton: Princeton University Press, 1979), pp. 127–32; Peter Vergo, "Kandinsky: Art Nouveau to Abstraction," in *Kandinsky: The Munich Years 1900–14: An Edinburgh International Fes-

A Note on the Translation

Kandinsky's interest in the possibilities of synthesis between painting and the word poses special problems to the translator of *Klänge*. The poems are characterized by a deliberate simplification of vocabulary—Kandinsky's language tends to be general rather than highly specific—and he often refuses to adhere to an accepted grammatical code. His punctuation is irregular: in *Hügel*, he writes of a "langen schwarzen, falten-losen Rock" ["a long smooth, black coat"].[17] He may (as he does in *Fagott*) change tense abruptly in midstream: "Da wußte man schon, daß durch die gänzlich leeren Straßen ein weißes Pferd ganz allein wandert" ["And they knew that through the totally empty streets a white horse is walking all alone"]. At other times, he may arbitrarily rearrange the order of words in a single sentence, as in *Wurzel*: "Das Licht des Abend-sternes um die angegebene Stunde kommt" ["The light of the evening star at the appointed hour comes"]. Often, as in the poems *Klänge* and *Wasser*, he leaves sentences incomplete. In other poems (notably *Fagott* and *Glocke*), he extends them beyond the limits of rhetorical probability.

Because attention to form is an issue of central significance in *Klänge*, it is critical to attempt to reproduce that surface of artifice which the poems maintain. Throughout *Klänge*, language and poetic form remain curiously simple and precise. Kandinsky's interest in patterns of repetition, alliteration, and rhyme typically involves multiple variations on a small, often apparently insignificant, group of phrases or sounds. The intro-ductory fragments of the poem *Im Wald* or the hypnotic rhythms of the verse *Hymnus* embody a conscious playing with a minimum of poetic materials. Kandinsky will often devise more complex plays on individual words. This tendency is manifested most ex-plicitly in *Unverändert*, where three words are "redefined" through clever syntactical dismemberment. The fragmentation of "Banane" to "Bann! Ahne!," "furchtbar" to "Furcht bar," and "Tinten" to "tin-ten" (the last of which undergoes translator's meta-morphosis to "tickling" and "ting-a-ling") has a less complicated counterpart in the dia-logue which opens the poem *Warum?*: "Keiner. / Einer? / Nein. / Ja!" ["No one. / One? /

---

tival Exhibition Organised by the Scottish Arts Council in Association with the Lenbachhaus (Edinburgh: Edin-burgh International Festival and Scottish Arts Council, 1979), pp. 4–10.

    17. The translator's specific problem here (as in many of the poems of *Klänge*) is to determine the relative importance of assonance and word order in the original verse. Literal translation of this phrase, of course, pro-duces a "long black, smooth coat." The relationship of the adjectives in German is based upon repetition of three main sounds (the *l*, the *a*, and the ending, *-en*). The closer affinity (through assonance, syllabic count, and the lack of usual punctuation) of the first two words of the original series, and the variation in the final word, help to justify a syntactical rearrangement in the English.

No. / Yes!"]. More conventional puns occur—on "fest" ["solid"] and "bange" ["alarmed"]—in the poems *Das* and *Abenteuer*.

Like the play on "Tinten," some of Kandinsky's syntactical jokes resist literal translation and must be refashioned. The variation on *hängen* in the poem *Vorhang* ("Der Vorhang hing") consequently becomes "a certain curtain hung"; the "Ein Stein" chant in *Bunte Wiese* diminishes into "one stone."

To heighten the reader's consciousness of a formalized poetic universe, Kandinsky occasionally introduces words of his own. Generally, these words pertain to the domain of color and function on a principle of paradox rather than one of denotative specificity: "braunweiß" ["brownwhite"], "rotblau" ["redblue"], and "scharfrot" ["sharp-red"] are examples. The verbal pyrotechnics of *Blick und Blitz* are not characteristic of Kandinsky, though other Expressionist poets (notably August Stramm and Dadaists such as Jean Arp and Hugo Ball) exercised an active interest in word inventions and collages.

KANDINSKY

SOUNDS

HILLS

A mass of hills of all the colors you can imagine or care to imagine. All different sizes, but the shapes always alike, i.e. just one: Fat at the bottom, puffed out around the sides, flatround up above. Just plain, ordinary hills, like the kind you always imagine and never see.

17

Among the hills winds a narrow path simply white, i.e. neither bluish, nor yellowish, neither turning into blue, nor into yellow.

In a long smooth, black coat that covers him all the way down to his heels, a man walks on this path. His face is pale, but on his cheeks are two red spots. His lips are just as red. He has a big drum hung around his neck and he is drumming.

The man walks in a very funny way.

Sometimes he runs and beats his drum with feverish, irregular strokes. Sometimes he walks slowly, perhaps absorbed in his thoughts and drums almost mechanically in a long drawn-out tempo: one . . . one . . . one . . . one . . . sometimes he stands stock still and drums like the little soft white toy rabbit that we all love so well.

This standing doesn't last long though.

The man is running again, beating his drum with feverish, irregular strokes.

As if utterly exhausted he lies there, the black man, all stretched out over the white path, among the hills of all colors. His drum lies beside him and the two drumsticks too.

He's standing up already. Now he'll start running again.

All this I have seen from above and beg you too to look on it from above.

19

SEEING

Blue, Blue got up, got up and fell.
Sharp, Thin whistled and shoved, but didn't get through.
From every corner came a humming.
FatBrown got stuck—it seemed for all eternity.
           It seemed. It seemed.
You must open your arms wider.
           Wider. Wider.

And you must cover your face with red cloth.
And maybe it hasn't shifted yet at all: it's just that you've shifted.
White leap after white leap.
And after this white leap another white leap.
And in this white leap a white leap. In every white leap a white leap.
But that's not good at all, that you don't see the gloom: in the gloom is where it is.
That's where everything begins . . . .
With a . . . . Crash . . . .

23

BASSOON

Very large houses suddenly collapsed. Small houses remained standing. A fat hard egg-shaped orange-cloud suddenly hung over the town. It seemed to hang on the pointed point of the steep spindly town hall tower and radiated violet.
A dry, naked tree stretched its quaking and quivering long branches into the deep sky. It was very black, like a hole in white paper. Its four little leaves quivered for a long time. But there was no sign of wind.

▷

But when the storm came and buildings with thick walls fell down, the thin branches didn't move. The little leaves turned stiff: as if cast out of iron. A flock of crows flew through the air in a straight line over the town. And suddenly again everything was still.

The orange-cloud disappeared. The sky turned piercing blue. The town yellow enough to make you cry.

And through this silence a single sound rang: hoofbeats. And they knew that through the totally empty streets a white horse is walking all alone. The sound lasted for a long time, a very, very long time. So no one knew exactly when it disappeared. Who knows when silence begins?

Through elongated, extended, somewhat expressionless, unsympathetic notes of a bassoon rolling far, far away deep in the distant emptiness, everything slowly turned green. First low and rather dirty. Then brighter and brighter, colder and colder, poisonous and more poisonous, even brighter, even colder, even more poisonous.

The buildings soared upward and became narrower. All of them leaned toward a point to the right, where perhaps the morning is.

It became perceptible as a striving toward morning.

And the sky, the houses, the pavement and the people who walked on the pavement became brighter, colder, more poisonously green. The people walked constantly, continually, slowly, always staring straight ahead. And always alone.

But the naked tree correspondingly grew a large, luxurious crown. This crown sat up high and had a compact, sausage-like shape that curved upward. The crown alone was so shrilly yellow that no soul would endure it.

It's good that none of the people walking below saw this crown.

Only the bassoon attempted to describe the color. It rose higher and higher, became shrill and nasal in its outstretched note.

How good that the bassoon couldn't reach this note.

27

OPEN

Now disappearing slowly in green grass.
Now sticking in grey muck.
Now disappearing slowly in white snow.
Now sticking in grey muck.
Lay long: big long black reeds.
Lay long.
Long reeds.
Reeds.
Reeds.

EARLY SPRING

A man on the street took off his hat. I saw black-and-white hair stuck down to the right and left of his part with hair cream.
Another man took off his hat. I saw a big pink, slightly greasy bald spot with a bluish highlight.
The two men looked at one another, each showing the other crooked, greyish yellowish teeth with fillings.

CAGE

It was torn in two. I took it in both hands and held the two ends together. Something grew all around. Close around me. But you couldn't see anything of it.

I thought there wasn't anything there. But still I couldn't go forward. I was like a fly inside a cheese bell.

I.e. nothing visible yet still impossible to overcome. It was even empty. In front of me, all alone, stood a tree, actually a sapling. Its leaves green, like verdigris. Dense like iron and just as hard. Little bloodshimmering red apples hung from its branches.

That was all.

THAT

You all know this giant cloud that's like the cauliflower. It lets itself be chewed snowwhitehard. And the tongue stays dry. That's how it weighed on the deep blue air.
And below, beneath it on the ground, on the ground stood a burning house. It was solid, oh, solidly built of dark red tiles.
And it stood in solid yellow flames.
And in front of this house on the ground . . .

BELL

Once in Weisskirchen a man said: . "I never, never do that."
At the exact same time in Mühlhausen a woman said: "Beef with horse-
radish."
Both of them said what they said, because there was no other way.
I hold a pen in my hand and write with it. I wouldn't be able to write with it if
it were out of ink.
The great big beast that took such joy in chewing its cud was knocked
senseless by quick, repeated, hollow-sounding hammer blows to the skull.
It sank down. An opening in its body let the blood run its course. Much
thick, sticky, smelly blood ran for an interminable time.

▷

With what wonderful skill they tore off the thick, warm, velvety hide covered with beautiful ornamental patterns of brownwhite hair. Skinned hide and red steaming odorful meat.
Very flat land, disappearing flat into all horizons.
Far to the left, a little birch grove. Still very young, soft white trunks and bare branches. Nothing but brown fields, carefully plowed in straight rows. In the middle of this giant circle a little village, just a few greywhite houses. Right in the middle a church steeple. The little bell is pulled by a rope and goes: ding, ding, ding, ding, ding . . . . . .

39

EARTH

The heavy earth was laid on carts with heavy spades. The carts were loaded and were heavy. The men shouted at the horses. The men cracked their whips. Heavily the horses pulled the heavy carts with the heavy earth.

WHY?

"No one came out of there."
"No one?
"No one.
"One?
"No.
"Yes! But when I came by, there was one standing there.
"At the door?
"At the door. He stretched out his arms.
"Yes! Because he doesn't want to let anyone in.
"No one came in there?
"No one.
"The one who stretched out his arms, was he there?
"Inside?
"Yes. Inside.
"I don't know. He just stretches out his arms so no one can get in.
"Was he sent there so No One can get in? The one who stretches out his arms?
"No. He came and stood there himself and stretched out his arms.
"And No One, No One, No One came out?
"No One, No One."

UNCHANGED

My bench is blue, but it's not always there. Only day before yesterday I found it again. Next to it stuck the cooled off flash of lightning, as always. This time the grass around the flash was slightly charred. Maybe the flash glowed suddenly in secret, with its point in the ground. Other than that, I could discern no change: everything in its old place. As always. I sat on my bench. To the right the flash in the ground — with its point sunk from sight: the one that perhaps glowed alone. In front of me the great plain. To my right fifty paces away the woman with the black cloth pressed to her breast, like a banana. She is looking at the red mushroom. To my left the same weather-beaten inscription:

"Ban! Anna!"

I have read it many times and knew from afar what sounded weather-beaten on this white board. As usual two hundred paces away from me the four little green houses grew out of the ground. Without a sound. The door of the second house from the left opened. The fat red-headed man in pale purple tights (when I see him I always think of the dropsy) led his spotted

▷

horse from the last house to the right on the hill, leaped on his back and (as the saying goes) rode off like the wind. As always his cry thundered fearfully in the distance:

"Just you wait! Ha! I'll pay you your fear full!"

Immediately then as always the gaunt Turk came out of the second house (from the right) with his white watering can, watered his dry little tree with colored inks, sat down, propped his back against the trunk and laughed. (I couldn't hear the laughing.) And I had the same crazy thought, that the colored inks were tickling him. Then, from a faraway, invisible bell came the sound

"ting-a-ling."

And the woman turned her face to me.

OBOE

Nepomuk had his beautiful new dress coat on when he sat himself down on the little round flat hill.
Down below the little blue green lake caught his eye.
Nepomuk leaned his back against the trunk of the little white green birch tree, pulled out his big long black oboe and played many beautiful songs which everybody knows. He played for a long time with deep feeling. Maybe going on two hours. Just as he started up with "There came a bird a-flying" and had gotten to "a-fly," Meinrad came running up the hill all hot and out of breath and with his crooked, pointed, sharp, curved, shining sword struck off a nice fat chunk of the oboe.

SPRINGTIME

Quiet, motley man!
Slowly the old house slips down the hill. The old blue sky is caught hope-
lessly between branches and leaves.
Don't call to me!

Sound hangs hopelessly in the sky, like a spoon in thick dough. Feet stick to the grass. And the grass wants to pierce the invisible with its blades. Raise the ax high over your head and chop! chop away!
Your words don't reach me. They hang like wet rags on the bushes.
Why won't anything grow, just this rotting wooden cross there at the crossroad? And its arms have pierced the air to the right and to the left. And its head has made holes in the sky. And from its edges creep strangling redblue clouds. And lightning rips and tears at them where you least expect it, and without a trace their cuts and gashes heal. And someone falls like a soft coverlet. And someone speaks, speaks — — — speaks — — —
Is it you again, you motley man? You again?

A THING OR TWO

A fish went deeper and deeper into the water. It was silver. The water blue. I followed it with my eyes. The fish went deeper and deeper. But I could still see it. I couldn't see it anymore. I could still see it, when I couldn't see it. Yes, yes I saw the fish. Yes, yes I saw it. I saw it. I saw it. I saw it. I saw it. I saw it. I saw it.

A white horse on long legs stood quietly. The sky was blue. The legs were long. The horse was motionless. Its mane hung down and didn't move. The horse stood motionless on its long legs. But it was alive. Not a twitch of a muscle, no quivering skin. It was alive.

Yes, yes. It was alive.

In the wide meadow grew a flower. The flower was blue. There was only one flower in the wide meadow.

Yes, yes, yes. It was there.

50

NOT

The jumping man interested me a great deal. He excited me. In the flat, hard, dry ground he dug a small very round depression and jumped over it without stopping every day from 4 o'clock to 5.—He jumped from one side of the depression to the other with an effort that would have gotten him over a hole three meters wide. And then right back over again.
And then right back over again. And right back over! Back over, back over! Oh, back over again, back over again! Back again, back again. Oh, back again, back again, back again. Ba-ackagain . . . Ba-ack-ckagain . . .

▷

One shouldn't look at such a thing.

But if you were already there, and if just for once, one single tiny time, then . . . yes, then . . . then how are you supposed to look away? How are you supposed to not go over? Not go? The not is sometimes impossible to reach. What person now living the second (and last) half of his life on earth this time doesn't know . . . Everybody knows! And that's why again and again I have to go back to the jumping man. And he excites me. He makes me sad. He . . .

Don't ever go there!! Don't ever look at him!! . . . . . . Never!! . . . . . .

. . . .

. . . .

. . . .

It's already past 3:30. I'm going over. Otherwise I'll be late.

55

STILL?

You, wild foam.
You, good-for-nothing snail, you who don't love me.
Empty silence of endless soldiers' steps, that here cannot be heard.
You, set of four windows with a cross in the middle.
You, windows of the empty hall, of the white wall where no one leans. You, speaking windows with inaudible sighs. You ignore me: you weren't built for me.

You, true mortar.

▷

You, meditative swallow, you who don't love me.

Self-consuming silence of rumbling wheels that chase and shape the figures.

You, thousands of stones that weren't laid for me and sunk down with hammers. You hold my feet in a spell. You are small, hard and gray. Who gave you the power to show me the glittering gold?

You, speaking gold. You wait for me. You invite me: you were built for me.
You, soulful mortar.

SOUNDS

Face.
Far.
Cloud.
. . . .
. . . .
There stands a man with a long sword. The sword is long and also broad.
Very broad.
. . . .
. . . .
He tried to trick me many times and I admit it: He succeeded too — at
tricking. And maybe too many times.
. . . .
. . . . .
Eyes, eyes, eyes . . . eyes.
. . . . .
. . . . .
A woman, who is thin and not young, who has a cloth on her head, which is
like a shield over her face and leaves her face in shadows.
With a rope the woman leads the calf, which is still small and unsteady on
its crooked legs. Sometimes the calf walks behind her very obediently.

▷

And sometimes it doesn't. Then the woman pulls the calf by the rope. It lowers its head and shakes it and braces its legs. But its legs are weak and the rope doesn't break.
The rope doesn't break.
. . . . .
. . . . .
Eyes look out from afar.
The cloud rises.
. . . . .
. . . . . .
The face.
Afar.
The cloud.
The sword.
The rope.

WATER

In the yellow sand walked a little thin red man. He was always slipping. It looked as if he walked upon an ice sheet. It was, however, yellow sand of the boundless plain.

From time to time he said: "Water . . . Blue water." And didn't understand himself why he said it.

A rider dressed in a green pleated coat rushed by on a yellow horse.

▷

The green rider drew his big white bow, turned around in his saddle and shot the arrow at the red man. The arrow whistled like a cry and wanted to force itself into the heart of the red man. At the last moment, the red man grasped it with his hand and threw it to one side.

The green rider smiled, bent over the neck of the yellow horse and disappeared into the distance.

The red man grew larger and his step became surer. "Blue water," he said. He walked on and the sand formed dunes and hard hills which were gray. The farther he walked, the harder, grayer, higher the hills, until finally cliffs began.

And he had to force himself in between the cliffs until he could neither stand still nor go back. You can't go back.

As he went by a very steep, pointed cliff, he noticed that the white man who was squatting up above wants to drop a big gray block on him. You couldn't go back. He had to go into the narrow passageway. And he went. Just as he got under the cliff, the man up above, with a gasping effort, gave the last shove.

And the block fell on the red man. He caught it on his left shoulder and tossed it behind him. — The white man up above smiled and nodded to him in a friendly fashion. — The red man grew even larger, i.e. taller. — — "Water, water," he said. — — The passageway between the cliffs grew wider and wider, until finally the flatter dunes came again and they became flatter and flatter, until they weren't there at all.

— Instead, nothing but a plain again.

IN TWO

The little man wanted to break the chain in two and of course he couldn't do it. The big man broke it very easily. The little man wanted to slip right through.
The big man held him by the sleeve, bent down and whispered in his ear: "we'll keep this to ourselves." And both of them laughed heartily.

DIFFERENT

Once there was a big 3 — white on dark brown. Its top curve was exactly the same size as its bottom one. At least that's what many people thought. And yet the top one was just a
little, little, little
bit bigger than the bottom one.

▷

This 3 always looked to the left — never to the right. And it also looked down a little bit, since the number only seemed to stand straight up. In reality, which wasn't easy to see, the top leaned just a
                    little, little, little
bit to the left.
So the big white 3 always looked to the left and just a tiny bit down.
But then again maybe it was different.

73

EXIT

You clapped your hands. Don't lean your head toward your joy.
Never, never.
And now he's cutting again with the knife.
Again he's cutting through with the knife. And now the thunder rolls in the
sky. Who led you in deeper?
In the dark deep quiet water the tops of the trees point down.
Always. Always.
And now he sighs. A heavy sigh. Again he sighed. He sighed.
And the stick hits against something dry.
Who then will point to the door, the exit?

IN THE WOODS

The woods grew deeper and deeper. The red trunks bigger and bigger. The green crowns heavier and heavier. The air darker and darker. The bushes lusher and lusher. The mushrooms thicker and thicker. Until there was nothing but mushrooms to walk on. It was harder and harder for the man to walk, to force his way through without slipping. But on he went anyway, repeating faster and faster and over and over the same sentence: — —

      The scars that mend.
      Colors that blend.

▷

To his left and slightly behind him walked a woman. Every time the man finished his sentence, she said with great assurance and rolling her r's vigorously:
verrry cleverrr.

82

83

CURTAIN

The rope went down and a certain curtain went up. We have all waited so long for this moment. A certain curtain hung. A certain curtain hung. A certain curtain hung. It was hanging down. Now it's up. When it went up (started up), we were all so very pleased.

WHITE FOAM

I'd like to know why it's like this and not different. It could be different, very, very different.
On a ravenblack horse a woman rides through flat green fields. I can't see the end of these fields. The woman is dressed in red, her face is hidden by a canaryyellow veil. The woman beats the horse without mercy. It just can't go any faster. Anyway it's already foaming and is growing whiter and whiter from the white hot foam. The woman sits up straight without swaying and beats the black horse.

Don't you think it would be better if the black horse could die? It's turning all white from the white hot foam!
But it can't die. Oh no! That it can't do.
How different it could be, how very different.

HYMN

Within, the bluish wavelet tosses.
The torn and shredded scarlet cloth.
Scarlet tatters. Deep blue wavelets.
The ancient book whose place is lost.
Looking silent in the distance.
Dark confusion in the wood.
Deeper grow the deep blue wavelets.
Scarlet cloth sinks down for good.

LATER

In the deep summit I know I will find you. Where smooth pricks. Where sharp doesn't cut. You hold the ring in your left hand. I hold the ring in my right hand. No one sees the chain. But these rings are the last links of the chain.

The beginning.
The end.

ADVENTURE

Once I visited a summer colony where no one lived. All the houses were neat and white and had green shutters that were tightly shut. In the middle of this summer colony was a green square, overgrown with grass. In the middle of this square stood a very old church with a tall belfry with a pointed roof. The big clock ran, but didn't strike. At the foot of this belfry stood a red cow with a very fat belly. It stood there without moving and chewed sleepily. Every time the minute hand of the clock pointed to a quarter-, a half-, or a full hour, the cow roared: "Oh! don't be so alarmed!" Then it went back to chewing again.

95

CHALK AND SOOT

Oh, how slowly he goes.
If only there were someone there who could say to the man: Faster, go faster, faster, faster, faster, faster.
But he's not there. Or is he?
This black face with its white lips, very white lips, as if they had been painted on, plastered on, powdered on with chalk.

▷

And the green ears!
Were they green? Or weren't they? Or were they?
Every Fall the trees lose their leaves, their dress, their jewels, their body, their crown.
Every Fall. And how many to go? How many Falls to go? Eternity? Or no? Or?
How slowly he goes.
And every Spring violets grow. And smell, smell. They always smell. Don't they ever stop smelling? Or do they? Would you rather he had a white face and black lips, as if they had been plastered on, painted on, powdered on with soot? Would you like that, better?
Or is there someone there who will say to the man and maybe is saying already: Faster, faster, faster.
Faster, faster, faster, faster, faster.

SPRING

1.

In the west the new moon.
Before the new moon's horn a star.
A tall thin black house.
Three lighted windows.
Three windows.

2.

There are pale blue spots on the yellow glare. Only my eyes saw the pale blue spots. They did my eyes good. Why didn't anyone see the pale blue spots on the yellow glare?

3.

Dip your fingers in the boiling water.
Scald your fingers.
Let your fingers sing the pain.

LEAVES

I can remember one thing.
A very tall triangular black mountain reached all the way up to the sky. Its silver tip was barely visible. To the right of this mountain stood a tree which was very thick and had a very thick green crown. This crown was so thick that it was impossible to separate one leaf from another. To the left on just one spot, but very close together, grew tiny white blossoms that looked like flat little plates.
Other than that there was nothing there.
I stood before this landscape and looked.

Suddenly a man came riding up from the right. He rode on a white goat, which looked perfectly normal, except that its horns were pointed forward instead of backward. And its tail didn't stick right up impudently the way it should, but hung down and was bare.

But the man had a blue face, a little pug nose. He laughed and showed his teeth which were small and wide apart, and looked worn down, but extremely white. I also noticed something sharp-red.

I was very surprised, because the man grinned at me.

He rode by slowly and disappeared behind the mountain.

It was strange too, that when I looked at the landscape again, all the leaves were lying on the ground and to the left there were no more flowers.

Instead only red berries.

The mountain, of course, remained motionless.

This time.

SONG

A man sits in
A narrow ring,
A narrow ring
Of thinness.
He is content.
He has no ear.
And doesn't have his eyeballs.
He cannot find
What's left behind
Of red sounds of the sun ball.
Whatever falls
Stands up again.
And what was dumb,
It sings a song.
Until the man,
Who has no ear,
And doesn't have his eyeballs,
Will start to find
Signs left behind
Of red sounds of the sun ball.

ROOT

Quick little spiders fled before my hand. Nimble little spiders. Your pupils reflected my eyes.

❖

— "Does he still remember the tree?
— "The birch tree?

❖

The light of the evening star at the appointed hour comes. Do you know when?

❖

— "The tree I saw he doesn't know.
— "The tree grows in growing from hour to hour.
— "And the fire destroys the dry leaves.
— "The dry leaves.

❖

▷

The bell tries to knock holes in the air.
And can't do it.
It is always caught.

— "He can remember the tree. The tree trembled from underneath, from its
roots, to up above, to its crown.
— "Oh!! the uppermost leaves.
— "He still remembers the tree!!
— "The birch tree?

TABLE

Once there was a long table. Oh, a long, long table. Right
and left at this table sat many, many, many people.
people, people,
people.
Oh, a long, long time at this long, long table sat people.

BRIGHT FIELD

In a field that had no grass, only flowers that were brightly colored, five men sat in a straight line.
A sixth one stood to the side.
  The first one said:
    "The roof is sound . . . Is sound the roof . . . Sound . . .

After a while the second one said:

"Don't touch me: I'm sweating . . . It's sweating I am . . . Yes!

And then the third one:

"Not over the wall!

Not over the wall! No!

But the fourth one:

"Ripening fruit!!

After a long silence the fifth one screamed in a shrill voice:

"Wake him up! Make his eyes big! A stone is rolling down the mountain. One, stone, one stone, a stone, a stone! . . . Down the mountain! . . . It's rolling down! . . . Make his ears greedy! Oh make his eyes big! Make his legs long! Long, long . . . his legs!!

The sixth one who stood to the side cried out short and loud:

"Silence!

LOOK

Why are you watching me through the white curtain? I didn't call after you, I didn't ask you to look through the white curtain at me. Why does it hide your face from me? Why can't I see your face behind the white curtain? Don't watch me through the white curtain! I didn't call after you. I didn't ask you. Through closed eyelids, I see how you watch me, when you watch through the white curtain. I'll pull back the white curtain and see your face, and you won't see mine. Why can't I pull back the white curtain? Why does it hide your face from me?

THE TOWER

Man in green tights with his turned up moustache lay almost outspread in
the green meadow. I never liked him. All around were red mushrooms.
Woman came out of the green forest. She was blue and disagreeable to me.
She sat down beside him and all the mushrooms disappeared.
Were gone.
Man stood up and went. And woman beside him. And they went out of the
green forest to the big red house.
The gray door was tightly shut. The door wasn't there.
She went inside. Then he went inside too.
Way up high on the tower both of them stand often, which is disagreeable.
The gray door is tightly shut.

SIGHT LIGHTNING

That as he (the man) sought nourishment, the dense white comb beat
down the rosebird. Now she rolls the windows wet in wooden cloths! —
Not to the faraway, but crooked. — The orchestra exploded — oh! oh! Half-
round purecircles press almost on chessboards and! books of iron! Kneel-
ing next to the jagged ox wants to Nürnberg wants to lie down — unbear-
able weight of the eyebrows. Heaven, heaven, printed bands you can
bear . . . From my head too the leg could grow from the short-tailed horse
with the pointed muzzle. But the redtacking, the yellowhacking at North-
pollacking like a rocket at
midday!

SOFTNESS

Each one lay on his own horse, which was unsightly and indecent. It's better even if a fat bird sits on a not his skinny branch with the little trembling leaping living leaf. Anyone can kneel (whoever can't, learns how). Can everyone see the spires? Open up! Or the fold will blow the roof off!

KANDINSKY

KLÄNGE

HÜGEL

Eine Masse von Hügeln in allen Farben, die sich einer denken kann und will. Alles verschiedene Größen, aber Formen immer gleich, d. h. nur eine: Dick unten, geschwollen an den Seiten, flachrund oben. Also einfache, gewöhnliche Hügel, wie man sie sich immer denkt und nie sieht.
Zwischen den Hügeln schlängelt sich ein schmaler Pfad einfach weiß, d. h. weder bläulich, noch gelblich, weder ins Blaue, noch ins Gelbe.
In einem langen schwarzen, faltenlosen Rock, welcher sogar die Fersen bedeckt, gekleidet, geht auf diesem Pfad ein Mann. Sein Gesicht ist blaß, aber auf den Backen sind zwei rote Flecken. Ebenso rot sind die Lippen. Er hat eine große Trommel umgehängt und trommelt.
Sehr komisch geht der Mann.
Manchmal läuft er und gibt seiner Trommel fieberhafte, unregelmäßige Schläge. Manchmal geht er langsam, vielleicht in seine Gedanken vertieft und trommelt fast mechanisch in einem lang gezogenen Tempo: eins . . . eins . . . eins . . . eins . . . manchmal bleibt er ganz stehen und trommelt wie das weichfellige weiße Spielhäschen, welches wir alle so lieben.
Dieses Stehen dauert aber nicht lange.
Da läuft der Mann schon wieder und gibt seiner Trommel fieberhafte, unregelmäßige Schläge.
Wie gründlich erschöpft liegt er da, der schwarze Mann, lang gestreckt auf dem weißen Pfad, zwischen den Hügeln in allen Farben. Seine Trommel liegt neben ihm und auch die zwei Schläger.
Er steht schon auf. Er wird schon wieder laufen.
Das alles habe ich von oben gesehen und bitte auch euch, von oben darauf zu schauen.

(Translation on page 17)

SEHEN

Blaues, Blaues hob sich, hob sich und fiel.
Spitzes, Dünnes pfiff und drängte sich ein, stach aber nicht durch.
An allen Ecken hat's gedröhnt.
Dickbraunes blieb hängen scheinbar auf alle Ewigkeiten.
Scheinbar. Scheinbar.
Breiter sollst du deine Arme ausbreiten.
Breiter. Breiter.
Und dein Gesicht sollst du mit rotem Tuch bedecken.
Und vielleicht ist es noch gar nicht verschoben: bloß du hast dich verschoben.
Weißer Sprung nach weißem Sprung.
Und nach diesem weißen Sprung wieder ein weißer Sprung.
Und in diesem weißen Sprung ein weißer Sprung. In jedem weißen Sprung ein weißer Sprung.
Das ist eben nicht gut, daß du das Trübe nicht siehst: im Trüben sitzt es ja gerade.
Daher fängt auch alles an . . . .
. . . . Es hat gekracht . . . .

(page 21)

FAGOTT

Ganz große Häuser stürzten plötzlich. Kleine Häuser blieben ruhig stehen.
Eine dicke harte eiförmige Orangewolke hing plötzlich über der Stadt. Sie schien an der spitzen Spitze des hohen hageren Rathausturmes zu hängen und strahlte violett aus.
Ein dürrer, kahler Baum streckte in den tiefen Himmel seine zuckenden und zitternden langen Äste. Er war ganz schwarz, wie ein Loch im weißen Papier. Die vier kleinen Blätter zitterten eine ganze Weile. Es war aber windstill.

Wenn aber der Sturm kam und manches dickmäuriges Gebäude umfiel, blieben die dünnen Äste unbeweglich. Die kleinen Blätter wurden steif: wie aus Eisen gegossen.

Eine Schar Krähen flog durch die Luft in schnurgerader Linie über der Stadt.

Und wieder plötzlich wurde alles still.

Die Orangewolke verschwand. Der Himmel wurde schneidend blau. Die Stadt gelb zum Weinen.

Und durch diese Ruhe klang nur ein Laut: Hufeisenschläge. Da wußte man schon, daß durch die gänzlich leeren Straßen ein weißes Pferd ganz allein wandert. Dieser Laut dauerte lange, sehr, sehr lange. Und man wußte deswegen nie genau, wann er aufhörte. Wer weiß, wann die Ruhe entsteht?

Durch gedehnte, lang gezogene, etwas ausdruckslose, teilnahmslose, lange, lange in der Tiefe sich im leeren bewegenden Töne eines Fagotts wurde allmählich alles grün. Erst tief und etwas schmutzig. Dann immer heller, kälter, giftiger, noch heller, noch kälter, noch giftiger.

Die Gebäude wuchsen in die Höhe und wurden schmäler. Alle neigten sie zu einem Punkt nach rechts, wo vielleicht der Morgen ist.

Es wurde wie ein Streben dem Morgen zu bemerkbar.

Und noch heller, noch kälter, noch giftiger grün wurde der Himmel, die Häuser, das Pflaster und die Menschen, die darauf gingen. Sie gingen fortwährend, ununterbrochen, langsam, stets vor sich schauend. Und immer allein.

Eine große, üppige Krone bekam aber dementsprechend der kahle Baum. Hoch saß diese Krone und hatte eine kompakte, wurstartige, nach oben geschweifte Form. Diese Krone allein war so grell gelb, daß kein Herz es aushalten würde.

Es ist gut, daß keiner der da unten gehenden Menschen diese Krone gesehen hat.

Nur das Fagott bemühte sich diese Farbe zu bezeichnen. Es stieg immer höher, wurde grell und nasal in seinem gespannten Ton.

Wie gut das ist, daß das Fagott diesen Ton nicht erreichen konnte.

(page 25)

OFFEN

Bald im grünen Gras langsam verschwindend.

Bald im grauen Kot steckend.

Bald im weißen Schnee langsam verschwindend.

Bald im grauen Kot steckend.

Lagen lange: dicke lange schwarze Rohre.

Lagen lange.

Lange Rohre.

Rohre.

Rohre.

(page 31)

VORFRÜHLING

Ein Herr nahm in der Straße seinen Hut ab. Ich sah schwarzweiße, fest mit Pomade rechts und links vom Scheitel klebende Haare.

Ein anderer Herr nahm seinen Hut ab. Ich sah eine große rosige, etwas fette Glatze mit bläulichem Glanzlicht.

Die beiden Herren sahen sich an, gegenseitig zeigten sie sich schiefe, gräulich gelbliche Zähne mit Plomben.

(page 32)

KÄFIG

Zerrissen war es. Ich nahm es mit beiden Händen und hielt die beiden Enden an einander. Ringsum wuchs etwas. Dicht um mich herum. Es war aber gar nichts davon zu sehen.

Ich dachte, es wäre auch nichts da. Aber doch konnte ich nicht vorwärts. Ich war wie eine Fliege in der Käseglocke.

D. h. nichts Sichtbares und doch unüberwindlich. Es war sogar leer. Ganz allein stand vor mir ein Baum, eigentlich ein Bäumchen. Die Blätter grün, wie Grünspan. Dicht wie Eisen und ebenso hart. Kleine blutleuchtende rote Äpfelchen hingen an den Zweigen.

Das war alles.

(page 33)

DAS

Ihr kennt alle diese Riesenwolke, die dem Carviol gleicht. Sie läßt sich schneeweißhart kauen. Und die Zunge bleibt trocken.

Also lastete sie auf der tiefblauen Luft.

Und unten, unter ihr auf der Erde, auf der Erde stand ein brennendes Haus. Es war aus dunkelroten Ziegelsteinen fest, oh, fest gebaut.

Und es stand in festen gelben Flammen.

Und vor diesem Haus auf der Erde . . .

(page 34)

GLOCKE

Einmal sagte ein Mann in Weißkirchen: . „nie, nie tu ich das".

Ganz genau zur selben Zeit sagte eine Frau in Mühlhausen: „Rindfleisch mit Meerretich."

Beide haben jeder seinen Satz gesagt, da es anders nicht ging.

Ich halte eine Feder in der Hand und schreibe mit ihr. Ich

würde mit ihr nicht schreiben können, wenn sie ohne Tinte wäre.

Das große starke Tier, welches viel Freude am Kauen und Wiederkauen hatte, wurde durch schnell auf einander folgende, dumpf klingende Hammerschläge auf den Schädel betäubt. Es sank nieder. Eine Öffnung im Leibe ließ freien Lauf dem Blut. Viel dickes, klebriges, riechendes Blut floss unendlich lange.

Wie wunderbar geschickt wurde die dicke, warme, samtne Haut mit braunweißen Haaren in schöner Ornamentik bedeckt heruntergerissen. Abgezogene Haut und rotes dampfendes geruchvolles Fleisch.

Sehr flaches, in allen Horizonten flach verschwindendes Land. Ganz links ein kleines Birkenwäldchen. Noch sehr junge, zarte weiße Stämme und kahle Äste. Lauter braune Felder, fein in geraden Streifen gepflügt. Mitten in diesem Riesenkreis ein kleines Dorf, nur ein paar grauweißer Häuser. Genau in der Mitte ein Kirchturm. Die kleine Glocke wird an der Schnur gezogen und macht: deng, deng, deng, deng, deng . . . . . .

(page 37)

ERDE

Die schwere Erde wurde mit schweren Spaten auf Fuhren gelegt. Die Fuhren wurden geladen und wurden schwer. Die Menschen schrien die Pferde an. Mit den Peitschen knallten die Menschen. Zogen schwer die Pferde die schweren Fuhren mit der schweren Erde.

(page 41)

WARUM?

,,Keiner ist da herausgekommen.''

,,Keiner?

,,Keiner.

,,Einer?

,,Nein.

,,Ja! Aber als ich vorbeikam, stand doch einer da.

,, Vor der Tür?

,,Vor der Tür. Er breitete die Arme aus.

,,Ja! Weil er niemanden hineinlassen will.

,,Keiner ist da hineingekommen?

,,Keiner.

,,Der, der die Arme ausbreitet, war der da?

,,Drin?

,,Ja. Drin.

,,Ich weiß nicht. Er breitet nur die Arme aus, damit keiner hinein kann.

,,Wurde er hingeschickt, damit Keiner hineinkann? Der die Arme ausbreitet?

,,Nein. Er kam und stellte sich selbst hin und breitete die Arme aus.

,,Und Keiner, Keiner, Keiner ist herausgekommen?

,,Keiner, Keiner.''

(page 42)

UNVERÄNDERT

Meine Bank ist blau, aber nicht immer da. Erst vorgestern habe ich sie wieder gefunden. Neben ihr steckte der abgekühlte Blitz, wie immer. Dieses Mal war das Gras um den Blitz herum etwas verbrannt. Vielleicht glühte der Blitz plötzlich im Geheimen, mit der Spitze in der Erde. Sonst fand ich keine Änderung: alles an der alten Stelle. Es war wie immer. Ich saß auf meiner Bank. Rechts der Blitz in der Erde — mit der Spitze versunken: er, der vielleicht allein glühte. Vor mir die große Ebene. Rechts fünfzig Schritt weit von mir die Frau mit dem schwarzen Tuch an die Brust gepreßt, wie eine Banane. Sie guckt auf den roten Pilz. Links von mir dieselbe verwitterte Inschrift:

,,Bann! Ahne!''

Ich habe es oft gelesen und wußte von weitem, was auf dieser weißen Tafel verwittert klingt. Wie gewöhnlich wuchsen zweihundert Schritte weit von mir die vier grünen Häuschen aus dem Boden heraus. Geräuschlos. Die Tür des zweiten von links ging auf. Der dicke rothaarige Mann in seinem blaßvioletten Trikot (immer denke ich an Wassersucht, wenn ich ihn sehe) zog sein scheckiges Pferd aus dem letzten Häuschen rechts am Hügel heraus, sprang darauf und ritt (wie man so sagt) wie der Wind davon. Wie immer donnerte furchtbar sein Geschrei von weitem:

,,Wart nur du! Ha! Ich zahle dir die Furcht bar!''

Dann kam sofort darauf wie immer aus dem zweiten Häuschen (von rechts) mit seiner weißen Gießkanne der hagere Türke heraus, begoß mit bunten Tinten sein dürres Bäumchen, setzte sich, lehnte den Rücken an den Stamm und lachte. (Das Lachen konnte ich nicht hören.) Und ich bekam denselben wahnsinnigen Gedanken, daß ihn die bunten Tinten kitzeln. Dann hörte man von einer weiten, unsichtbaren Glocke das

,,tin-ten''

schlagen. Und die Frau wendete zu mir ihr Gesicht.

(page 45)

HOBOE

Nepomuk hatte seinen schönen neuen Gehrock an, als er sich auf dem kleinen runden flachen Hügel niederließ.
Unten stach der kleine blaue grüne See die Augen.
Nepomuk lehnte sich an den Stamm der kleinen weißen grünen Birke an, zog seine große lange schwarze Hoboe heraus und spielte viele schöne Lieder, die jedermann kennt. Er spielte sehr lange mit sehr viel Gefühl. Vielleicht an die zwei Stunden. Als er gerade ,,Es kam ein Vogel geflogen" anfing und zum ,,geflo . . ." kam, so lief ganz erhitzt und außer Atem Meinrad den Hügel herauf und schlug mit seinem krummen, spitzen, scharfen, gebogenen, glänzenden Säbel ein gutes Stück von der Hoboe ab.

(page 47)

FRÜHLING

Schweig du, bunter Mensch!
Langsam rutscht vom Hügel das alte Haus. Der alte blaue Himmel steckt hoffnungslos zwischen Ästen und Blättern.
Ruf mich nicht hin!
Hoffnungslos bleibt in der Luft das Läuten hängen, wie der Löffel im dicken Brei. Die Füße pappen am Gras. Und das Gras will das Unsehbare mit seinen Spitzen durchstechen. Heb hoch das Beil über dem Kopfe und hau! Hau doch!
Deine Worte erreichen mich nicht. Da hängen sie wie nasse Lumpen an den Büschen.
Warum wächst nichts, nur dieses hölzerne faulende Kreuz da am Scheidewege? Und seine Arme haben die Luft nach rechts und nach links durchgestochen. Und sein Haupt hat den Himmel durchlöchert. Und kriechen von den Rändern erwürgende rotblaue Wolken. Und Blitze reißen und schneiden sie da, wo du sie am wenigsten erwartest, und spurlos heilen ihre Stiche und Schnitte. Und jemand fällt wie en weiches Oberbett. Und jemand spricht, spricht — — — spricht — — —
Bist das wieder du, du bunter Mensch? Wieder du?

(page 48)

EINIGES

Ein Fisch ging immer tiefer ins Wasser. Er war silbern. Das Wasser blau. Ich verfolgte ihn mit den Augen. Der Fisch ging immer tiefer. Ich sah ihn aber noch. Ich sah ihn nicht mehr. Ich sah ihn noch, wenn ich ihn nicht sehen konnte.
Doch, doch ich sah den Fisch. Doch, doch ich sah ihn. Ich sah ihn. Ich sah ihn. Ich sah ihn. Ich sah ihn. Ich sah ihn. Ich sah ihn.

Ein weißes Pferd auf hohen Beinen stand ruhig. Der Himmel war blau. Die Beine waren hoch. Das Pferd war unbeweglich. Die Mähne hing herunter und bewegte sich nicht. Das Pferd stand unbeweglich auf den hohen Beinen. Es lebte aber doch. Kein Muskelzucken, keine zitternde Haut. Es lebte.
Doch, doch. Es lebte.
Auf der breiten Wiese wuchs eine Blume. Die Blume war blau. Es war nur eine Blume auf der breiten Wiese.
Doch, doch, doch. Sie war da.

(page 50)

NICHT

Der springende Mann interessierte mich sehr. Er regte mich auf. Er hat in die flache, harte, trockene Erde eine kleine sehr runde Vertiefung gegraben und sprang unaufhörlich jeden Tag von vier bis fünf Uhr darüber.—Er sprang von einer Seite der Vertiefung auf die andere mit einer Anstrengung, die für ein drei Meter langes Loch reichen würde. Und sofort wieder zurück.
Und sofort wieder zurück. Und sofort zurück! Zurück, zurück. Oh! wieder zurück, wieder zurück! Wieder, wieder. Oh wieder, wieder, wieder. Wi-ieder . . . Wi-iede-er . . .
So etwas sollte man nicht mit-ansehen.
Wenn man aber schon da war, wenn auch nur einmal, ein einziges kleines Mal, dann . . . ja, dann . . . wie soll man dann die Augen davon abwenden? Wie soll man nicht hingehen? Nicht hingehen? Das nicht ist manchmal unmöglich zu erreichen. Wer von den Menschen, welche die zweite Hälfte (und letzte) ihres Lebens auf Erden diesesmal leben, weiß nicht . . . Jeder weiß! Und darum muß ich immer wieder hin zum springenden Mann. Und er regt mich auf. Er macht mich traurig. Er . . . Geh nie hin!! Sieh' ihn nie an!! . . . . . . Nie!! . . . . . .
. . . .
. . . .
. . . .

Es ist schon nach halb vier. Ich gehe hin. Sonst komme ich zu spät.

(page 53)

DOCH NOCH?

Du, wilder Schaum.
Du, nichtsnutzige Schnecke, die du mich nicht liebst.
Leere Stille der unendlichen Soldatenschritte, die ich hier nicht hören kann.
Ihr, vier Quadratfenster mit einem Kreuz in der Mitte.
Ihr, Fenster des leeren Saales, der weißen Mauer, an die sich

keiner anlehnte. Ihr, erzählende Fenster mit unhörbaren Seuf-
zern. Ihr seid mir kaltzeigend: nicht für mich seid ihr gebaut.

Du, wahrer Leim.

Du, vieldenkende Schwalbe, die du mich nicht liebst.

Sich verschluckende Stille der rollenden Räder, die die Ge-
stalten jagen und schaffen.

Ihr, tausende von Steinen, die nicht für mich gelegt werden
und mit Hammern versenkt. Ihr haltet meine Füße im Banne.

Ihr seid klein, hart und grau. Wer hat euch die Macht gege-
ben, mir das glänzende Gold zu zeigen?

Du, erzählendes Gold. Du wartest auf mich. Du bist mir warm-
zeigend: für mich bist du gebaut.

Du, seelischer Leim.

(page 57)

KLÄNGE

Gesicht.
Ferne.
Wolke.

. . . .

. . . .

Es steht ein Mann mit einem langen Schwert. Lang ist das
Schwert und auch breit. Sehr breit.

. . . .

. . . .

Er suchte mich oft zu täuschen und ich gestehe es: Das ge-
lang ihm auch — das Täuschen. Und vielleicht zu oft.

. . . .

. . . . .

Augen, Augen, Augen . . . Augen.

. . . . .

. . . . .

Eine Frau, die mager ist und nicht jung, die ein Tuch auf dem
Kopf hat, welches wie ein Schild über dem Gesichte steht
und das Gesicht im Schatten läßt.

Die Frau zieht am Strick das Kalb, welches noch klein ist und
wacklig auf den schiefen Beinen. Manchmal läuft das Kalb
hinterher ganz willig. Und manchmal will es nicht. Dann zieht
die Frau das Kalb am Strick. Es beugt den Kopf und schüt-
telt ihn und stämmt die Beine. Aber die Beine sind schwach
und der Strick reißt nicht.

Der Strick reißt nicht.

. . . . .

. . . . .

Augen schauen aus der Ferne.

Die Wolke steigt.

. . . . .

. . . . . .

Das Gesicht.
Die Ferne.
Die Wolke.
Das Schwert.
Der Strick.

(page 61)

WASSER

Im gelben Sand ging ein kleiner dünner roter Mann. Er rutschte
immer aus. Es schien, daß er auf Glatteis geht. Es war aber
gelber Sand der grenzenlosen Ebene.

Von Zeit zu Zeit sagte er: „Wasser . . . Blaues Wasser". Und
verstand selbst nicht, warum er das sagte.

Ein im grünen faltigen Rock angezogener Reiter ritt auf einem
gelben Pferd rasend vorbei.

Der grüne Reiter spannte seinen dicken weißen Bogen, drehte
sich im Sattel um und schoß den Pfeil auf den roten Mann.

Der Pfeil pfiff, wie Weinen und wollte sich ins Herz des roten
Mannes hineinzwingen. Der rote Mann nahm ihn im letzten
Augenblick mit der Hand und schmiß ihn zur Seite.

Der grüne Reiter lächelte, beugte sich an den Hals des gelben Pferdes und verschwand in der Ferne.

Der rote Mann ist größer geworden und sein Schritt wurde
fester. „Blaues Wasser" sagte er.

Er ging weiter und der Sand bildete Dünen und harte Hügel,
die grau waren. Je weiter desto härtere, grauere, höhere Hügel
bis endlich Felsen anfingen.

Und er mußte zwischen den Felsen sich durchzwingen, da
er weder stehen bleiben konnte, noch zurück gehen. Zurück
kann man nicht.

Als er an einem sehr hohen, spitzen Felsen vorbei ging, so
merkte er, daß der oben hockende weiße Mensch einen dicken
grauen Block auf ihn fallen lassen will. Zurück konnte man
nicht. Er mußte in den engen Gang. Und er ging. Gerade als
er unter dem Felsen war, gab der Mann da oben mit schnau-
fender Mühe den letzten Hieb.

Und der Block fiel auf den roten Mann. Er fing ihn mit seiner
linken Schulter auf und schmiß ihn hinter seinen Rücken. —

Der weiße Mann oben lächelte und nickte freundlich mit dem
Kopf. — Der rote Mann wurde noch größer, d. h. höher. — —

„Wasser, Wasser" sagte er. — — Der Gang zwischen den Felsen wurde immer breiter, bis endlich wieder flachere Dünen
kamen, die noch flacher wurden und noch flacher, so daß sie

überhaupt nicht da waren.
— Sondern nur wieder eine Ebene.

(page 65)

DER RISS

Der kleine Mann wollte die Kette zerreißen und konnte natürlich nicht. Der große Mann zerriß sie ganz leicht. Der kleine Mann wollte sofort durchschlüpfen.
Der große Mann hielt ihn am Ärmel, beugte sich zu ihm und sagte leise in's Ohr:
„das müssen wir verschweigen". Und sie lachten beide von Herzen.

(page 68)

ANDERS

Es war eine große 3 — weiß auf dunkelbraun. Ihr oberer Haken war in der Größe dem unteren gleich. So dachten viele Menschen.
Und doch war dieser obere
                              etwas, etwas, etwas
größer, als dieser untere.
Diese 3 guckte immer nach links — nie nach rechts. Dabei guckte sie auch etwas nach unten, da die Zahl nur scheinbar vollkommen gerade stand. In Wirklichkeit, die nicht leicht zu bemerken war, war der obere
                              etwas, etwas, etwas
größere Teil nach links geneigt.
So guckte diese große weiße 3 immer nach links und ein ganz wenig nach unten.
Es war vielleicht auch anders.

(page 71)

AUSGANG

Du hast in die Hände geklatscht. Neig' nicht deinen Kopf zu deiner Freude.
Nimmer, nimmer.
Und da schneidet er wieder mit dem Messer.
Wieder schneidet er mit dem Messer durch. Und da rollt der Donner am Himmel. Wer führte dich tiefer ein?
Im dunklen tiefen ruhigen Wasser sind die Bäume mit den Spitzen nach unten.
Immer. Immer.
Und da seufzt er. Ein schwerer Seufzer. Wieder seufzte er.
Seufzte er.
Und da schlägt der Stock auf etwas trockenes.
Wer zeigt da die Tür, den Ausgang?

(page 75)

IM WALD

Der Wald wurde immer dichter. Die roten Stämme immer dicker. Die grünen Kronen immer schwerer. Die Luft immer dunkler. Die Büsche immer üppiger. Die Pilze immer zahlreicher. Man mußte schließlich auf lauter Pilze treten. Es war dem Mann immer schwerer zu gehen, sich durchzudrängen, nicht auszurutschen. Er ging aber doch und wiederholte immer schneller und immer denselben Satz: — —
            Die heilenden Narben.
            Entsprechende Farben.
Links von ihm und etwas hinter ihm ging eine Frau. Jedesmal als der Mann mit seinem Satz fertig wurde, sagte sie sehr überzeugt und das „r" stark rollend:
sehrrr prrraktisch.

(page 79)

VORHANG

Der Strick ging nach unten und der Vorhang ging nach oben. Auf diesen Augenblick haben wir alle schon so lange gewartet. Der Vorhang hing. Der Vorhang hing. Der Vorhang hing. Er hing noch unten. Jetzt ist er oben. Als er nach oben ging (zu gehen anfing), haben wir uns alle so sehr gefreut.

(page 85)

WEISSER SCHAUM

Ich möchte gern wissen, wozu das so ist und nicht anders. Anders könnte das sein, ganz, ganz anders.
Auf einem rabenschwarzen Pferd reitet eine Frau durch flache grüne Wiesen. Ich kann das Ende dieser Wiesen nicht sehen. Die Frau ist rot angezogen, das Gesicht ist durch kanariengelbe Schleier verhüllt. Die Frau schlägt erbarmungslos das Pferd. Es kann ja doch nicht schneller laufen. Es saust ja ohnehin und wird immer weißer durch weißen heißen Schaum. Die Frau sitzt gerade und wackelt nicht und schlägt das schwarze Pferd.
Glaubt Ihr nicht, daß es besser wäre, wenn das schwarze Pferd sterben könnte? Es wird ja ganz weiß vom weißen heißen Schaum!
Es kann aber nicht sterben. Oh nein! Das kann es nicht.
Wie anders das sein könnte, ganz anders.

(page 86)

HYMNUS

Innen wiegt die blaue Woge.
Das zerrissne rote Tuch.
Rote Fetzen. Blaue Wellen.

Das verschlossne alte Buch.
Schauen schweigend in die Ferne.
Dunkles Irren in dem Wald.
Tiefer werden blaue Wellen.
Rotes Tuch versinkt nun bald.

(page 88)

SPÄTER

In der tiefen Höhe finde ich dich schon. Dort wo das Glatte sticht. Dort wo das Scharfe nicht schneidet. Du hältst den Ring in der linken Hand. Ich halte den Ring in der rechten Hand. Keiner sieht die Kette. Aber diese Ringe sind die letzten Glieder der Kette.

Der Anfang.
Das Ende.

(page 91)

ABENTEUER

Einmal besuchte ich eine Villenkolonie, wo niemand lebte. Alle Häuser waren schmuckweiß und hatten festgeschloßne grüne Läden. In der Mitte dieser Villenkolonie war ein grasbewachsener grüner Platz. In der Mitte dieses Platzes stand eine sehr alte Kirche mit einem hohen Glockenturm mit spitzem Dach. Die große Uhr ging, schlug aber nicht. Am Fuße dieses Glockenturmes stand eine rote Kuh mit einem sehr dicken Bauch. Sie stand unbeweglich und kaute schläfrig. Jedesmal, wenn der Minutenzeiger an der Uhr eine Viertel-, Halbe- oder Ganzestunde zeigte, brüllte die Kuh: „ei! sei doch nicht so bange!" Dann kaute sie wieder.

(page 92)

KREIDE UND RUSS

Oh, wie langsam er geht.
Wenn nur einer da wäre, der dem Menschen sagen könnte: Schneller, geh doch schneller, schneller, schneller, schneller, schneller.
Er ist aber nicht da. Oder doch?
Dieses schwarze Gesicht mit den weissen Lippen, ganz weißen Lippen, wie mit Kreide angestrichen, angeschmiert, angeschminkt.
Und die grünen Ohren!
Waren sie grün? Oder doch nicht? Oder doch?
Die Bäume verlieren jeden Herbst ihr Laub, ihr Kleid, ihren Schmuck, ihren Körper, ihre Krone.
Jeden Herbst. Und wieviel noch? Wieviel Herbste noch? Ewigkeit? Oder nicht? Oder doch?
Wie langsam er geht.

Und jedes Frühjahr wachsen Veilchen. Und duften, duften. Immer duften sie. Hören sie nie auf zu duften? Order doch?
Möchtest du lieber, er hätte ein weißes Gesicht und schwarze Lippen, wie mit Ruß angeschmiert, angestrichen, angeschminkt? Möchtest du das, lieber?
Oder ist doch einer da, der dem Menschen sagen wird und vielleicht schon sagt: Schneller, schneller, schneller.
Schneller, schneller, schneller, schneller, schneller.

(page 97)

LENZ

1.

Im Westen der neue Mond.
Vor des neuen Mondes Horn ein Stern.
Ein schmales hohes schwarzes Haus.
Drei beleuchtete Fenster.
Drei Fenster.

2.

Auf der gelben Grelligkeit sind blaßblaue Flecken. Bloß meine Augen sahen die blaßblauen Flecken. Wohl taten sie meinen Augen. Warum hat keiner die blaßblauen Flecken gesehen auf der gelben Grelligkeit?

3.

Tauche deine Finger in das siedende Wasser.
Verbrühe deine Finger.
Laß deine Finger vom Schmerz singen.

(page 104)

BLÄTTER

Ich kann mich einer Sache erinnern.
Ein sehr großer dreieckiger schwarzer Berg reichte bis zum Himmel. Kaum sichtbar war seine silberne Spitze. Rechts von diesem Berge stand ein Baum, welcher sehr dick war und eine sehr dicke grüne Krone hatte. Diese Krone war so dick, daß die einzelnen Blätter nicht von einander zu trennen waren. Links wuchsen nur auf einem Fleck, aber sehr dicht, kleine weiße Blüten, die wie flache Tellerchen aussahen. Sonst war nichts da.
Ich stand vor dieser Landschaft und guckte.
Auf einmal kommt von rechts ein Mann geritten. Er ritt auf einem weißen Ziegenbock, welcher ganz gewöhnlich aussah, hatte aber die Hörner nicht nach hinten gerichtet, sondern nach vorne. Und sein Schwanz stand nicht wie sonst

frech nach oben gedreht, sondern hing nach unten und war
kahl.

Der Mann aber hatte ein blaues Gesicht, eine kurze Stumpf-
nase. Er lachte und zeigte seine kleinen, weit von einander
stehenden, ziemlich abgebrauchten, aber doch sehr weißen
Zähne. Etwas scharfrotes habe ich auch bemerkt.

Sehr erstaunt war ich, da der Mann mich angrinste.

Er ritt langsam vorbei und verschwand hinter den Berg.

Sonderbar war dabei, daß als ich wieder auf die Landschaft
guckte, so lagen alle Blätter auf den Boden und links waren
keine Blumen mehr. Sondern bloß rote Beeren.

Der Berg blieb freilich unbeweglich.

Diesesmal.   (page 108)

LIED

Es sitzt ein Mann
Im engen Kreis,
Im engen Kreis,
Der Schmäle.
Er ist vergnügt.
Er hat kein Ohr.
Und fehlen ihm die Augen.
Des roten Schalls
Des Sonnenballs
Er findet keine Spuren.
Was ist gestürzt,
Das steht doch auf.
Und was nicht sprach,
Das singt ein Lied.
Es wird der Mann,
Der hat kein Ohr,
Dem fehlen auch die Augen
Des roten Schalls
Des Sonnenballs
Empfinden feine Spuren.   (page 110)

WURZEL

Bewegliche kleine Spinnen flohen vor meiner Hand. Kleine
flinke Spinnen. Meine Augen wurden von deinen Pupillen zu-
rückgeworfen.

— „Entsinnt er sich noch des Baumes?"

— „Der Birke?"

Das Licht des Abendsternes um die angegebene Stunde
kommt. Weißt du wann?

— „Den Baum, den ich gesehen habe, kennt er nicht.

— „Der Baum wächst im Wachsen von Stunde zu Stunde.

— „Und die Flamme zerstört das dürre Laub.

— „Das dürre Laub.

Die Glocke sucht Löcher in die Luft zu schlagen.

Und kann es nicht.

Immer ist sie gefangen.

— „Des Baumes kann er sich entsinnen. Der Baum erzitterte
von unten, von der Wurzel, bis oben, bis zur Krone.

— „Oh!! die obersten Blätter.

— „Noch entsinnt er sich des Baumes!!

— „Der Birke?"   (page 111)

TISCH

Es war ein langer Tisch. Oh, ein langer, langer Tisch. Rechts
und links an diesem Tische saßen viele, viele, viele Menschen,
Menschen, Menschen,
Menschen.

Oh, lange, lange saßen an diesem langen, langen Tische
Menschen.   (page 113)

BUNTE WIESE

Auf einer Wiese, auf der kein Gras war, sondern nur Blumen,
die höchst bunt waren, saßen in gerader Linie fünf Männer.
Ein sechster stand seitwärts.

Der erste sagte:

„Das Dach ist fest . . . Ist fest das Dach . . . Fest . . .

Nach einer Weile sagte der zweite:

„Rühr mich nicht an: Ich schwitze . . . Schwitzen tu ich
. . . Ja!

Und dann der dritte:

„Nicht über die Mauer!

Nicht über die Mauer! Nein!

Der vierte aber:

„Reifende Frucht!!

Nach langem Schweigen schrie der fünfte mit greller
Stimme:

„Weckt ihn! Macht ihm die Augen groß! Es rollt ein Stein
vom Berge. Ein, Stein, ein Stein, ein Stein, ein Stein! . . .
Vom Berge! . . . Er rollt herunter! . . . Macht ihm die Ohren
gierig! Oh macht ihm die Augen groß! Macht ihm die Beine
lang! Lang, lang . . . die Beine!!

Der sechste, der seitwärts stand schrie auf kurz und stark:

„Schweigen!

(page 114)

BLICK

Warum schaust du auf mich durch den weißen Vorhang? Ich rief nicht nach dir, ich bat dich nicht, durch den weißen Vorhang zu schauen auf mich. Wozu verbirgt er dein Gesicht vor mir? Warum sehe ich nicht dein Gesicht hinter dem weißen Vorhang? Schau nicht auf mich durch den weißen Vorhang! Ich rief nicht nach dir. Ich bat dich nicht. Durch die geschlossenen Lider sehe ich, wie du auf mich schaust, da du durch den weißen Vorhang schaust. Ich ziehe den weißen Vorhang zur Seite und werde dein Gesicht sehen, und du wirst meins nicht sehen. Warum kann ich nicht den weißen Vorhang zur Seite ziehen? Wozu verbirgt er dein Gesicht vor mir?

(page 116)

DER TURM

Mann im grünen Trikot mit seinem nach oben gedrehten Schnurrbart lag fast ausgebreitet auf der grünen Wiese. Ich mochte ihn nie. Rote Pilze waren ringsum.
Frau kam aus dem grünen Walde heraus. Blau war sie und mir unangenehm.
Sie setzte sich neben ihm und alle Pilze verschwanden. Waren weg.
Mann stand auf und ging. Und Frau neben ihm. So gingen sie aus dem grünen Walde auf das große rote Haus zu.
Die graue Tür war fest verschlossen. Die Tür war nicht da.
Sie ging hinein. Dann ging er auch hinein.
Auf dem Turm ganz hoch oben stehen sie beide oft, was un-
angenehm ist.
Die graue Tür ist fest verschlossen.

(page 117)

BLICK UND BLITZ

Daß als sich er (der Mensch) ernähren wollte, entschlug der dichte weiße Kamm den Rosavogel. Nun wälzt sie die Fenster naß in hölzernen Tüchern! — Nicht zu den entfernten, aber krummen. — Entlud sich die Kapelle — ei! ei! Halbrunde Lauterkreise drücken fast auf Schachbretter und! eiserne Bücher! Kniend neben dem zackigen Ochs will Nürnberg will liegen — entsetzliche Schwere der Augenbrauen. Himmel, Himmel, bedruckte Bänder du ertragen kannst . . . Auch aus meinem Kopf könnte vom kurzschwänzigen Pferde mit Spitzmaul das Bein wachsen. Aber der Rotzacken, der Gelbhacken am Nordpollacken wie eine Rakete am
Mittag!

(page 118)

DAS WEICHE

Jeder lag auf seinem eigenen Pferde, was unschön und unanständig war. Es ist schon jedenfalls besser, wenn ein dicker Vogel auf einem nicht seinem dünnen Ast sitzt mit dem kleinen zitternden bebenden lebenden Blatt. Jeder kann knien (wer nicht kann, der lernt es). Kann jeder die Spitztürme sehen? Tür auf! Oder die Falte reißt das Dach weg!

(page 119)

WASSILY KANDINSKY
A Chronology

I am indebted here to Kandinsky's *Reminiscences* (originally published as "Rückblicke" in *Kandinsky, 1901–1913* [Berlin: Der Sturm, 1913]), trans. Mrs. Robert L. Herbert, in *Modern Artists on Art: Ten Unabridged Essays,* ed. Robert L. Herbert (Englewood Cliffs, N.J.: Prentice-Hall, 1964), pp. 19–44, and to Will Grohmann's *Wassily Kandinsky: Life and Work*, trans. Norbert Guterman (London: Thames & Hudson, 1959). References are to these editions by page.

EARLY YEARS

1866   Kandinsky born in Moscow, December 4.
1869   Parents spend a year in Italy. Kandinsky attends kindergarten in Florence.
1871   Family moves to Odessa on account of father's health. Kandinsky attends *gymnasium*. Drawing lessons.

MOSCOW YEARS 1886–96

1886   Begins study of political economy and law at the University of Moscow, where he becomes interested in peasant law. Here, he notes in *Reminiscences,* he gains "practice in 'abstract' thinking" (p. 25).
        Paints in spare time (primarily church interiors in Moscow).

1889   Sent to Vologda province to report on peasant laws.
        Drawings; discovery of folk art; studies of peasant architecture and decoration.
        Visits the Hermitage in Petersburg where he admires Rembrandt's chiaroscuro.
        Hears Wagner's *Lohengrin* and becomes convinced that painting can develop the same power as music (*Reminiscences* p. 26).
1892   Passes law examinations at Moscow.
        Marries cousin, Ania Chimiakin.
1893   Appointed lecturer, University of Moscow.
1895   Visits French Impressionist exhibition in Moscow and is profoundly affected by one of Monet's Haystack paintings, in which he at first recognizes no objective forms.
        Manages a printing shop which deals in reproductions.
1896   Offered professorship at University of Dorpat, but declines, effectively relinquishing his academic career. Moves to Munich to study painting.

MUNICH YEARS 1897–1908

1897–99 Enrolls at Anton Ažbè's school in Munich. Produces drawings.

Disillusionment with studio work (drawing from nature, anatomical drawings). Regarded as a "colorist." Fails drawing examination for Munich Academy.

Meets Alexej von Jawlensky.

1900 Studies with Stuck at the Munich Academy.

Munich becomes German center of Jugendstil movement. Van de Velde speaks of the force and independence of the abstract line (*Kunstgewerbliche Laienpredigten* [Lay sermons on the arts and crafts], 1902).

1900–08 Development of graphic work; strong romantic and traditional elements in both woodcuts and paintings (Rococo, Biedermeier, Jugendstil); becomes skilled at realistic representation.

Foundation of many new periodicals encourages dissemination of artistic ideas.

1901 Founds Phalanx group, for which he executes a Jugendstil-style poster.

Drawings of nudes and anatomy; landscape sketches from nature; costume designs.

1901–03 Introduced to philosophy of Rudolf Steiner, the theosophist.

Research into technical aspects of painting (testing of media and paints).

1902 Becomes president of Phalanx. Teaches at Phalanx School, where Gabriele Münter is one of his pupils.

1902–03 Landscape studies; color and disposition of forms become increasingly less realistic.

1903 Engagement to Gabriele Münter.

Phalanx School closes. Travels in Italy and Russia.

1904 Phalanx group disbands. Travels to Holland and Odessa. Extended stay in Tunisia.

Tempera paintings. Publishes first collection of woodcuts, *Stikhi bez slov* [Poems without words].

1904–05 Awarded medals in Paris.

1905 Goes to Odessa. Exhibits at Salon d'Automne and Indépendants, Paris. Extended stay at Rapallo.

Fauves exhibit at Salon d'Automne; Die Brücke founded in Dresden.

1906 Spends one year at Sèvres, near Paris. Publishes *Xylographies*, a collection of woodcuts.

1907 Travels to Switzerland. Returns to Munich in the summer. September 1907 to April 1908 in Berlin.

Period of intellectual and psychological doubt.

Indépendants shows Matisse's *Bonheur de vivre*, which provokes much protest.

1908 Returns to Munich. Rest cure at Reichenhall. Begins to spend summers at Murnau, in Upper Bavaria. First Murnau sketches.

MURNAU PERIOD 1908–10

1908–09 Transitional years. Kandinsky is "overflowing with energy" (Grohmann, p. 56); color begins to figure centrally in his painting.

1909 Buys house in Murnau.

Spirited talks about art with Jawlensky. With Jawlensky, founds Neue Künstlervereinigung, with Kandinsky as first president. Increasing contact with painters.

Affirms commitment to nonobjective painting: "Now I [know] for certain that the object [harms] my paintings" (*Reminiscences*, p. 32).

Composes *Der gelbe Klang* [The yellow sound], *Schwarz und Weiß* [Black and white], and *Grüner Klang* [Green sound], abstract pieces for the stage; probably writes the first poems for *Klänge*.

Murnau landscapes; first *Improvisations*.

1910 Meets Franz Marc.

Writes *Über das Geistige in der Kunst* [Concerning the spiritual in art]. Travels in Russia.

First *Komposition*.

Exhibitions of the Neue Künstlervereinigung raise furor in Munich. Kandinsky regards art of most members as "decorative" and derivative.

BLAUE REITER PERIOD 1911–13

1911   Kandinsky resigns from chairmanship of Neue Künstlervereinigung under pressure from other members who believe that his work is becoming too abstract; Marc, Kubin, and Münter follow.

Meets Arp, Klee, and Macke. With Franz Marc, founds Blaue Reiter. First Blaue Reiter exhibition; includes works of Kandinsky, Marc, Macke, Delaunay, Rousseau, and Schönberg.

Probably writes *Violett*, a composition for the stage (fragment published in *Bauhaus* 3:6 [1927]).

Kandinsky divorces Ania Chimiakin.

1912   Piper Verlag publishes *Über das Geistige in der Kunst*.

Second Blaue Reiter exhibition (with works by Arp, Klee, Kubin, Malevich, Picasso, and others).

Neue Küstlervereinigung dissolves.

Travels to Russia.

Delaunay's "Orphism"; first Futurist exhibition in Paris.

Publication of *Klänge*.

Publication of *Blaue Reiter Almanach* [Blue rider almanac], edited by Kandinsky and Franz Marc. Contains Kandinsky's dramatic piece, *Der gelbe Klang*.

1913   Participates in Armory Show, New York.

Exhibits in Germany. Publishes first version of "Rückblicke" [Reminiscences] in Berlin.

Beginning of Malevich's Suprematism. Tatlin's first Constructivist relief.

YEARS IN RUSSIA 1914–21

1914   Work interrupted by war; does not paint again until 1916. Spends three months on Lake Constance, where he writes the notes to *Punkt und Linie zu Fläche* [Point and line to plane], then travels to Odessa and Moscow.

1915   Spends three months in Stockholm with Gabriele Münter.

1916   Separates from Gabriele Münter. Returns t Moscow. Meets Nina Andreevskaya.

Swiss Dada movement begins in Zurich.

1917   Marries Nina Andreevskaya, February 11.

Hugo Ball lectures on Kandinsky at Galerie Dada.

1918   Appointed member, Commissariat for Publi Instruction (Division of Fine Arts). Teaches at Art School (Government A Workshops). Concern with pedagogica and institutional reform.

Publishes second version of "Rückblicke" (*Tekst Khudozhnika)* in Moscow.

Is discouraged, despite attention to the wo of Malevich and Tatlin, by the artistic situation in Moscow—it is no longer a source of inspiration to him.

1919   Founds Museum for Pictorial Culture. Estab lishes twenty-two new provincial museums.

Walter Gropius merges the Weimar School of Creative Art and the School of Industrial Arts to form the Bauhaus.

1920   Appointed professor, University of Moscow

1921   Executes *Bunter Kreis*, the first of his paintings composed almost entirely of clearly delineated shapes.

Founds Russian Academy of Aesthetics an becomes its vice-president.

Departs Russia on a three-month leave of absence and, when he fails to return, loses Russian citizenship. Arrives in Berlin, late December.

Dada Almanach appears; Dadaists become highly popular but hold little direct interest for Kandinsky.

BAUHAUS YEARS 1922–33

1922   Difficult winter. Moves to Weimar to teach at Bauhaus with Klee.

"Cool" period of geometrical, objective paintings.

1924   Weimar Bauhaus closes under attack from populace; Kandinsky denounced as "communist" and "dangerous agitator."

Blue Four (Kandinsky, Klee, Feininger, and Jawlensky) forms; exhibitions and sales of works in the United States.

1924–25   Period of interest in the circle.

Birth of Surrealism.

1925   Kandinsky moves to Dessau with the Bauhaus. His work is interrupted for a year.

The Bauhaus incorporates, significantly enlarging the scope of its activities.

1926   Kandinsky's sixtieth birthday. Exhibitions of his work held throughout Germany.

Publication of *Punkt und Linie zu Fläche*.

Father dies at Odessa.

1928   Kandinsky becomes a German citizen.

His production of Mussorgsky's *Pictures at an Exhibition* is performed at Dessau.

Continuing concern with the synthesis of art.

Resumes summer travels (eventually visiting Yugoslavia and the Near East).

1929   Compositions become increasingly polymorphous.

Exhibits in Paris, Brussels, Antwerp, The Hague, Basel, and the United States. Works bought by museums, though dealers still demonstrate a preference for Kokoschka, Beckmann, and Die Brücke.

1932   Anhalt government closes Bauhaus in Dessau. Kandinsky moves, with the Bauhaus, to Berlin.

1933   Freies Bauhaus closed by Nazi government. Kandinsky goes to Paris.

PARIS YEARS 1934–44

1934   Settles in Neuilly-sur-Seine. Though Parisian painters maintain their distance, he meets leading foreign artists, among others, Miró, Chagall, Pevsner, Magnelli, Brancusi, Ernst, and Mondrian. Friendships with Léger, Arp, and Delaunay.

Kandinsky enjoys rapidly growing international renown, but political circumstances make it impossible for him to exhibit extensively abroad.

At outbreak of war, artistic community dissolves. Léger, Chagall, and Mondrian go to the United States; Arp removes to Switzerland. Kandinsky remains in France.

Essays on the cultural significance of abstract art.

Paintings begin to lose "constructivist" features.

1937   Travels to Switzerland and visits the ailing Klee.

Nazi confiscations and exhibitions of "degenerate art." Fifty-seven of Kandinsky's works are confiscated and sold.

1944   Becomes ill in March; dies of sclerosis in the cerebellum, December 13. Buried in Neuilly.

Plans for a ballet and a film comedy remain uncompleted.

OTHER PUBLISHED SOURCES
OF KANDINSKY'S POETRY

Since the publication of *Klänge* in 1912, selections have appeared infrequently in anthologies and journals, often accompanied by poems of Kandinsky's later Parisian period (1933–44). A list of the sources of these poems, arranged in order of publication, appears below. It cannot claim to be exhaustive.

Poshchechina obshchestvennomu vkusu: stikhi, proza, stat'i [A slap in the face of public taste: poems, prose, articles]. Moscow: privately printed by G. L. Kuz'min, 1912, pp. 81–83. In this famous Russian futurist anthology, four poems from *Klänge*— *Käfig, Sehen, Fagott,* and *Warum?*—appeared in Russian (without Kandinsky's consent) alongside works of Livshits, Maiakovskii, Khlebnikov, Kruchenykh, and David and Nicolai Burliuk. Kandinsky later protested vehemently against his inclusion in the publication, with whose tone he could not sympathize. See Troels Andersen, "Some Unpublished Letters by Kandinsky," *Artes* 2 (Copenhagen, 1966): 96–97. The pieces here are described as "four little stories from his book *Klänge.*"

Almanach des Verlages, 1904–1914. Munich: Piper, 1914, pp. 157–59. In Piper's almanac, a reprint of the poem *Klänge.*

Cabaret Voltaire, no. 1 (May 1916), p. 21. This first publication of the Zurich Dada contains two poems from *Klänge, Blick und Blitz* and *Sehen.*

Kandinskii, V. V. *Tekst Khudozhnika.* Moscow: Izdanie Otdela Izobrazitel'nikh Iskusstv Narodnogo Kommissariata po Prosveshcheniiu, 1918, p. 5. In the second version of "Rückblicke," the poem *Sehen* appears in Russian.

Zehder, Hugo. *Wassily Kandinsky.* Dresden: Rudolf Kaemmerer, 1920, p. 7. Contains *Sehen* (here entitled *Blaues, Blaues*) from *Klänge.*

Einstein, Carl, and Paul Westheim, eds. *Europa-Almanach,* vol. 1. 1925. Reprint. Nendeln, Liechtenstein: Kraus, 1973, p. 65. Undated poem *Zwielicht.*

Transition, no. 27 (April-May 1938), pp. 104–09. Contains, along with three woodcuts, two poems from *Klänge, Blick und Blitz* and *Anders,* and in addition the poems *Ergo* (Paris, May 1937), *S* (Paris, May 1937), *Erinnerungen* (Paris, March 1937), and *Immer Zusammen* (Paris, May 1937).

Plastique 4 (1939): 14–16. [Reprinted in *Plastique, Nos. 1–5,* ed. Hans Arp et al. New York: Arno, 1969.] Poems from the Paris years: *Salongespräch* (June 1936), *Testimonium Paupertatis* (March 1937), and *Weiss-Horn* (May 1937).

'Abstrakt/Konkret'' Bulletin der Galerie des Eaux Vives Zürich, no. 8 (1945). Contains one poem from Klänge, Sehen (here entitled Blaues, Blaues), and two later poems, Testimonium Paupertatis and Weiss-Horn.

Kandinsky, Wassily.] Kandinsky: 11 Tableaux et 7 Poèmes. Amsterdam: Duwaer, 1945. Poems written in Paris: Viribus unitis (March 1937), Weiss-Horn, Testimonium Paupertatis, Salongespräch, Midi (Neuilly, March 1940), Les Promenades (January 1939), and Lyrique (March 1939).

Giedion-Welcker, Carola, ed. Poètes à l'Ecart; Anthologie der Abseitigen. Bern-Bümpliz: Benteli, 1946, pp. 53–60. Contains four poems from Klänge: Fagott, Anders, Blick und Blitz, and Sehen. Also included are Testimonium Paupertatis, S, Weiss-Horn, and Immer Zusammen.

Kandinsky, Wassily. "Prose Poems (1912–1937)." Translated by Ralph Manheim. In Concerning the Spiritual in Art, and Painting in Particular, 1912. New York: Wittenborn, Schultz, 1947, pp. 79–91. Fagott, Anders, Blick und Blitz, and Sehen, from Klänge, appear here for the first time in English translation, along with the following poems from Kandinsky's Parisian period: Testimonium Paupertatis, S, Weiss-Horn, Immer Zusammen, and Ergo. Poems and translations are arranged on facing pages.

Seuphor, Michel. L'Art abstrait, ses origines, ses premiers maîtres. Paris: Maeght, 1949, pp. 167–69. Selected poems: Les Promenades, Lyrique, Weiss-Horn, Salongespräch. Translated into French by Michel Seuphor.

Bill, Max, ed. Wassily Kandinsky. Paris: Maeght, 1951, pp. 89–93. Contains one poem from Klänge, Bunte Wiese, an untitled poem (signed Paris, February 8, 1936), and two additional poems, Und das Ende? (Paris, June 1, 1936), and Le Fond (Paris, July 1938).

Kandinsky, Wassily.] "Un poème inédit de Kandinsky." XXe Siècle 3 (June 1952): 72. The poem Midi.

Platschek, Hans, ed. Dichtung moderner Maler. Wiesbaden: Limes, 1956, pp. 39–49. Four selections from Klänge: Wasser, Im Wald, Kreide und Russ, and Der Turm.

Malende Dichter—Dichtende Maler. [Exhibition catalogue.] Kunstverein St. Gallen, 3 August–20 Oktober 1957. Zurich: Verlag der Arche, 1957, p. xli. Contains a reproduction of Kandinsky's manuscript of the poem Hoboe from Klänge.

Scheidegger, Ernst. Malende Dichter—dichtende Maler. Zurich: Verlag der Arche, 1957, pp. xli and 85. A reprinting of the catalogue from the Kunstverein St. Gallen exhibition. Includes a reproduction of the manuscript of Hoboe and a reprinting of Blick und Blitz from Klänge.

Schifferli, Peter, ed. Dada. Die Geburt des Dada. Dichtung und Chronik der Gründer. Zurich: Verlag der Arche, 1957, p. 83. Blick und Blitz from Klänge.

Staempfli, Edward. "Divertimento nach Gedichten von Hans Arp, Wassily Kandinsky und Paul Klee für Sopran und acht Instrumente." [Unpublished musical score.] (Berlin, July 1957– March 1958.) One poem by Klee, three poems by Arp, and Kandinsky's Weiss-Horn set to music.

Gegenklänge: Aquarelle und Zeichnungen von Wassily Kandinsky. Cologne: M. DuMont Schauberg, 1960, pp. 41, 49, and 55. Immer Zusammen, Testimonium Paupertatis, and Weiss-Horn are reprinted here from Carola Giedion-Welcker's anthology.

Wassily Kandinsky: Watercolors, Drawings, Writings. Translated by Norbert Guterman. London: Thames & Hudson, 1961, pp. 41, 49, and 55. A translation of Gegenklänge. Immer Zusammen, Testimonium Paupertatis, and Weiss-Horn appear here in English, translated by Ralph Manheim.

Schifferli, Peter, ed. Das war Dada: Dichtungen und Dokumente. Munich: DTV, 1963, p. 94. One poem from Klänge, Blick und Blitz.

Kandinsky, V. Poèmes illustrés de bois gravés originaux. Edited by Jean Cassou. Geneva, 1968.

(Limited edition of 100 copies.) Four poems from *Klänge* in French translation: *Abenteuer, Warum?, Frühling,* and *Kreide und Russ.*

Roethel, Hans Konrad. *Kandinsky: Das graphische Werk.* Cologne: M. DuMont Schauberg, 1970. Poems from *Klänge* (in facsimile) include *Vorfrühling, Hoboe, Einiges, Vorhang, Der Riss, Abenteuer,* and, appearing in part only, *Hügel, Unverändert, Doch Noch?, Klänge, Im Wald, Weisser Schaum, Kreide und Russ, Lenz, Blätter,* and *Bunte Wiese.* This is the definitive catalogue of Kandinsky's graphic work: it contains all of the woodcuts from *Klänge.*

Kandinsky, Wassily. *Regards sur le passé et autres textes, 1912–1922.* Edited by Jean-Paul Bouillon. Paris: Hermann, 1974, pp. 212–21. Six poems from *Klänge—Fagott, Anders, Bunte Wiese, Tisch, Blick und Blitz,* and *Sehen*—accompanied by French translations by Jean-Paul and Elisabeth Bouillon.

Kandinsky, Wassily. *Tutti gli scritti.* Milan: Giangiacomo Feltrinelli, 1974. Vol. 2, *Dello spirituale nell'arte, Scritti critici e autobiografico, Teatro,*

Poesie. Edited and with an introduction by Phillipe Sers. Translated by Libero Sosio, Nilo Pucci, and Brita and Enrico Chilò, pp. 332–74; 377–99. The poems of *Klänge* appear here in Italian translation by Libero Sosio, accompanied by the German text and selected woodcuts. Poems from 1936 to 1939 (in Italian translation only) are appended: *Zwielicht, Weiss-Horn, Salongespräch, Unzulänglich* (Paris, July 28, 1936), *Und das Ende?, Von-Zu* (Paris, August 2, 1936), *Erinnerungen, Viribus Unitis, Testimonium Paupertatis, Ergo, S, Immer Zusammen, Le Fond, Les Promenades, Lyrique, Précaution* (Paris, March 1939), *Le Sourd qui entend* (Paris, March 1939), *Midi,* and one untitled, undated poem.

Reed, Orrel P., Jr. *German Expressionist Art: The Robert Gore Rifkind Collection: Prints, Drawings, Illustrated Books, Periodicals, Posters.* Los Angeles: Frederick S. Wight Art Gallery, UCLA, 1977, pp. 110–13. Five poems from *Klänge* translated into English by Kate Steinitz: *Fagott, Sehen, Wasser, Käfig,* and *Vorfrühling.*